WHY DO MEN
LEAVE THE
SEAT UP?

WHY DO MEN
LEAVE THE
SEAT UP?

APANDISIS
α
PUBLISHING

Apandisis Publishing
105 Madison Avenue, Suite 3A
New York, New York 10016

ISBN-13: 978-1-4127-5274-9
ISBN-10: 1-4127-5274-4

Manufactured in USA

8 7 6 5 4 3 2 1

www.FYIanswers.com

Contents

Chapter Three
LOVE AND LUST

Chapter Four
ANIMAL KINGDOM

Chapter Five
PEOPLE

Chapter Six
BODY SCIENCE

Chapter Seven
FOOD AND DRINK

Chapter Eight
WEIRD SCIENCE AND TECHNOLOGY

Chapter Nine
HISTORY

Chapter Ten
SPORTS

Chapter Eleven
EARTH AND SPACE

Chapter Twelve
PLACES

Chapter One

HEALTH MATTERS

Q Why do men leave the seat up?

A Ever since Eve bit the apple, human history has been a battle between the sexes. But it wasn't until the late eighteenth century that men and women were given the weapon they needed to turn the battle into a war: In 1775, Alexander Cummings invented the flush toilet. Since then, the toilet seat has done more damage to marriages than strip clubs, charge cards, and mothers-in-law combined. Men and women each make a convincing argument in the Great Toilet Seat Debate. Men ask: Why should we always be responsible for putting the seat up and down? Shouldn't women *raise* the toilet seat when they're finished?

Women counter: We already do enough work around the house, and the disgusting risk of sitting on a urine-damp rim (or worse, falling into the toilet) far outweighs the minor inconvenience of raising and lowering a toilet seat. Why can't men simply put the seat down?

At first blush, the answer seems obvious: Men are inherently lazy. But perhaps what women consider "lazy," men call "efficient."

Indeed, some biologists argue that a number of human attributes have developed from the evolutionary imperative to conserve energy. These include a little trait known as bipedalism. This "energy efficiency" paradigm argues that the conservation of energy is necessary and beneficial to the survival of mankind. So it's possible that men leave the toilet seat up because they are conserving energy for the next evolutionary step of humankind. We don't know what this next step will be exactly, but it will undoubtedly involve a couch and a flat-screen TV.

Well, great. This explanation, however, does nothing for the woman whose nighttime trip to the bathroom is fraught with peril. Fortunately, whenever such a dilemma is raised (or lowered), you can bet it's been the subject of an academic paper.

Sure enough, several academicians have addressed the issue. Richard Harter, a retired mathematician from South Dakota (the mathematics business apparently is slow in South Dakota), tackled the problem in a 1998 paper. After factoring such variables as the likelihood of the woman agreeing to raise the toilet seat when she's finished ("none"), Harter concluded the most efficient and fair solution is for the man to put the seat down exactly half the time. In 2007, economist Hammad Al-Sabah Siddiqi, from the

Lahore University of Management Sciences in Pakistan, jumped into the fray. Siddiqi argued that because of wifely nagging, the social norm is to leave the toilet seat down, despite this being far less efficient than leaving it up.

There seems to be no end in sight to the battle of bathroom behavior. Too bad. If the sexes could forge a toilet-seat truce, they could focus on something really important: bickering about the in-laws.

Q What is the worst way to die?

A The psychologist Ernest Becker posited that we're so preoccupied with cheating death that we don't actually live, in a meaningful sense anyway. His suggestion is that the worst type of death is one that follows an insignificant life. This sounds like a load of bull to us, and we'd rather live an insignificant life with a relatively painless death than, say, be consumed in a fire or devoured by hungry piranhas.

Speaking of wasting large amounts of time thinking about death, some people do it as a career—they're known as thanatologists. Some journalists also have spent a lot of effort on the subject, including Anna Gosline, who wrote a long article for *The New Scientist* in 2007 in which she established two things: First, there are a lot of nasty ways to die; and second, she is a most curious person who would not be our first choice to take out to dinner, but who might be fun on Halloween.

Gosline's summary of a range of common painful deaths is magisterial. Here's a sampling of her findings:

- Bleeding to death. This was the Roman aristocracy's favorite form of suicide. The Romans would crawl into a warm tub, nick a vein, and slowly be carried off to the afterlife, full of self-righteous satisfaction at having thumbed their noses at the disagreeable emperors who were infringing on their wealthy prerogatives. Weakness, thirst, anxiety, dizziness, and confusion are common stages before unconsciousness from blood loss—but then, that sounds like a normal day for many of us.

- Burning to death. As in frat houses and newsrooms, it's the toxic gases that get most victims. But those who die directly from a fire's flames suffer immensely, as the inflammatory response to burns only increases the pain.

- Decapitation. Unless it's a botched job—as with Margaret Pole, the Countess of Salisbury, who fought her executioner in 1541 and was hit eleven times with the axe before succumbing—this seems relatively painless. Full-on death occurs in no more than seven seconds, when the brain's oxygen is used up. Of course, that means you would live for a few seconds after the blow, though that's only scientific speculation. Headless focus-group subjects are hard to rustle up.

- Falling. Like drowning, this no doubt frightens many people the most, because it can happen in the course of everyday life. Survivors have reported the sensation of time slowing down, and feeling alert and focused on maintaining an upright position and landing feet-first—an instinct we share with cats and other animals.

- Hanging. Apart from the awful dread that can only build from the moment you realize the jig is up, this is relatively quick and painless—unless the hangman's a hack and your fall is too short or the noose is poorly tied, in which case the struggle at the end of the rope is mighty uncomfortable.

Okay, we've had just about enough of this disconcerting topic, and we didn't even touch on crucifixion, lethal injection, the electric chair, and many other forms of death, natural and unnatural. Our personal un-favorite is an airplane crash, but frankly, we're too darned terrified of such a scenario to discuss it. Maybe Anna Gosline is free.

Q Can you really starve a fever and feed a cold?

A This folk remedy of yore (as well as its variation: feed a fever, starve a cold) isn't exactly medically sound advice. But it is more effective than using leeches to suck out an infection or throwing someone into water to see if she is a witch.

The earliest known reference to starving a fever comes from a 1574 book written by John Withals, whose main gig was writing dictionaries. He wrote, "Fasting is a great remedie of feuer." (We're unsure why a dictionary writer would fancy himself a doctor, but that's another story.) The feeding-a-cold bit must have been added, as this advice was passed from generation to generation.

But does it work? Eh, kind of. Generally, fevers cause a loss of appetite anyway, and your body can divert the energy that would have gone to digestion to fight the fever. A study conducted by Dutch scientists at the Academic Medical Center in Amsterdam found that fasting can help the body fight fever-causing bacteria. It also found that eating food helps boost the immune system, which fights the viruses that cause the common cold. But that's mainly beneficial before you get a cold. Once you catch a cold, you have a cold—period.

However, if you have a fever but are hungry, eat! Starvation is just not medically sound advice, particularly if your body is telling you that it wants food. And hydration is always extremely important, no matter what type of illness you have.

So, if you have a cold and you want some of your grandma's choc-olate cake, just give her the old adage, "Starve a fever and feed a cold!" Hopefully, she won't remember those words when you come down with a fever later on and tell her there is no sound scientific proof that having chocolate cake (and maybe some ice cream, too) will reduce your chances of getting better.

Q Where does Viagra come from?

A From a pharmacy. Duh. Actually, the medical marvel Viagra was discovered by accident.

A group of scientists at a laboratory in Kent, England, were working on a treatment for the heart condition angina. The scientists, employed by the drug corporation Pfizer, experimented with different molecules to treat angina, which is caused by restricted blood flow to the heart. One promising molecule—sildenafil—increased blood flow by blocking an enzyme called phosphodiesterase. As with most research, the details are complicated, but by the early 1990s, Pfizer began conducting clinical trials on men in Europe and the United States. Sildenafil worked—but not as intended.

Besides helping the heart, increased blood flow can engorge the penis and produce rock-hard, long-lasting erections. The men in the clinical trials gleefully reported this unexpected side effect to the scientists, who told their supervisors about it. Marketers at Pfizer realized very quickly that they had stumbled onto something *big* (pun intended). Angina research? *Forgetaboutit!* Sildenafil was tweaked to target the penis.

An eager market awaited sildenafil, which would be packaged as a little blue pill called Viagra. Most cases of erectile dysfunction (ED) occur because the penis is not getting enough blood. With older men, the arteries often aren't dilating enough. Fully half of men over age forty experience ED at least once in a while.

Viagra debuted in 1998 and became the fastest-selling drug in American history. International sales topped a billion dollars the next year. In 2003, rival drugs Cialis and Levitra entered the ED market. They also block phosphodiesterase, and Cialis has the added benefit of working for up to thirty-six hours.

Still, it is Viagra that has become synonymous with the treatment of erectile dysfunction. Viagra is to ED medications what Band-Aid is to adhesive bandages.

Q What did they use for birth control in the old days?

A Tough question. It's not information that got written down—at least not often.

Some hints are found in the ancient writings of doctors and naturalists. They show that fruits and herbs played a big role in controlling fertility. An Egyptian scroll of medical advice that's thirty-five hundred years old tells how to end a pregnancy at any point: Mix the unripe fruit of acacia with honey and other items to be soaked up by an absorbent pad of plant fiber; insert the pad into the vagina, and an abortion will follow. (Dissolved acacia produces lactic acid, which is a spermicide.)

Other old texts show that herbal birth control was brewed into teas. The leaves of pennyroyal (a type of mint) and parts of many plants that look like weeds to us could be brewed as a "morning-after" cure for unwanted pregnancies. Juniper berries, willow bark, mugwort, aloe, anise, dittany, and certain ferns were all used. Seeds from the plant Queen Anne's lace or from pomegranates were eaten for the same reason, as were figs. Many of these plant-based solutions were known to people in the Middle Ages and the Renaissance. In Shakespeare's *Hamlet,* Ophelia plays with the herb rue, a weed known to induce abortion. Rue is found throughout the Americas, too, and many native groups used it to end pregnancies.

What about condoms, sponges, and other devices? Illustrations thousands of years old show men using condoms, though the earliest condom found dates to 1640. It's made of sheep intestines. Goodyear began mass production of rubber condoms in 1843.

Female condoms, or cervical dams, have also been around for millennia. They've included seedpods, oiled paper, seaweed, lemon or pomegranate halves, beeswax, and even moss. History records the use of spermicidal potions made from oils, vinegar, rock salt, wine, and herbs.

Superstition and ignorance about the properties of certain ingredients played roles in some of these birth-control methods. Modern research on animals shows that some of these ingredients would have resulted in lower pregnancy rates or increased instances of miscarriage. However, some of these substances also are toxic, which would have made the birth-control benefits moot.

Q Is it dangerous to awaken a sleepwalker?

A We've all had the experience of waking up in the middle of the night to find ourselves drinking a Slurpee and singing Barry Manilow's "Copacabana" while stark naked on the back porch of the neighbor's house. Wait, everybody has, right? Er, we meant that metaphorically.

Sleepwalking, or somnambulism, is one of the great medical mysteries. Anyone who has encountered a sleepwalker wandering around the house—or singing naked on the back porch—can attest that it is an eerie experience. Sleepwalking is listed in a group of sleep disorders known as parasomnia, and researchers aren't sure what causes it. They know that stress and irregular sleep patterns may contribute to episodes, and that children are far more likely to suffer from the condition than adults. They also know that the old wives' tale warning that a person awakened from a somnambulist daze may die is just that—an old wives' tale.

Some experts trace this myth back to the beliefs of various indigenous cultures that thought when a person slept, his or her soul left the body, and that if you woke up a sleepwalker, the soul would be lost forever. Others argue that the myth arose simply due to the distress and shock sleepwalkers sometimes experience when woken up.

Though it is true that a sleepwalker may be distressed and disoriented upon being roused from a midnight stroll, there are no documented cases of sleepwalkers expiring from it. Indeed, sleep experts argue that not waking a sleepwalker can be more dangerous than waking one, especially if he or she is engaged in certain activities at the time (climbing, jumping, handling a knife, running the American government, etc.). In most cases, specialists suggest that it is best to gently guide the somnambulist back to bed.

There might be another reason to wake a sleepwalker. In 1982 an Arizona man named Steven Steinberg went on trial for killing his wife, who was stabbed twenty-six times with a kitchen knife. Despite overwhelming evidence and Steinberg's own admission that he had committed the crime, the defendant was unable to answer the simplest questions about the circumstances of his wife's death. Why? The man had killed his wife while sleepwalking. Steinberg was acquitted of the charges.

Q What happens if you don't drink eight glasses of water a day?

A If you follow the news, you know that the medical community tends to flip-flop on some of its assertions. High doses of vitamin E supplements, which had long been praised for their antioxidant qualities, have recently been linked to a higher incidence of death. And for years we were told to avoid sunlight with the strictness of vampires, only to find out recently that the vitamin D produced from sunlight—through exposure of only ten to fifteen minutes a few times a week—can strengthen our bones and decrease our risk of certain cancers. The latest reconsideration by MDs strikes at the age-old belief that eight glasses of water a day will lead to better health.

Some of the supposed health benefits of water made sense, at least to lay people. First, water was believed to help purify the body. Drinking a lot of water, after all, makes you pee, and urination is one way the body expels toxins. Furthermore, many doctors thought that if you filled up on water, you would be less likely to cram another Twinkie into your mouth.

Yes, the logic looked solid, but it apparently isn't based on scientific fact. A study published in a 2008 issue of the *Journal of the American Society of Nephrology* showed that athletes and people living in hot climates can benefit from an increased water intake, but there is no evidence that the recommended eight glasses of water a day has substantial health benefits for anyone else. While the researchers found that drinking more water would help the body clear out substances like sodium and urea, they pinpointed no clinically known benefit from this process. They saw no measurable correlation between water intake and weight maintenance.

The good news is that the researchers found that drinking eight glasses of water a day won't hurt you. Of course, this might change when the next study is published.

Q Is it true that listening to Mozart makes a baby smarter?

A That depends on your definition of smarter. When researchers in a 1993 study had participants listen to a Mozart sonata, they found that those people scored slightly higher on spatial-reasoning tests for about ten or fifteen minutes. That's what the researchers tested, that's all they claimed, and their methods seemed sound.

But within a year, the New York Times wrote an article in which it summarized, cheekily, that "listening to Mozart actually makes you smarter," and we were off to the races. In 1997, Don Campbell published a book called The Mozart Effect: Tapping the Power of Music to Heal the Body, Strengthen the Mind, and Unlock the Creative Spirit. Then came Campbell's The Mozart Effect for Children. Brand extensions of this powerful franchise are available to this day.

If the New York Times piece showed the suggestive power of the media, Campbell's books demonstrated the power of parental love. Here was a chance for a new generation of über-parents to achieve several desirable things simultaneously: They could help their kids become smarter, give them culture, and assuage their own residual guilt for having listened to Iron Maiden when they were young and impressionable.

Few separate studies have corroborated the limited findings of the original research. Other researchers have argued that Mozart doesn't make listeners smarter—it simply puts them in a better mood, which can translate to temporarily better scores on certain kinds of tests. Mozart's music also has been shown to cause significant—though again temporary—decreases in brain activity that leads to epileptic seizures.

In other words, there is little doubt that Mozart's music—considered to be both abstractly complex and aurally ingratiating—has a fleeting positive effect on people. But does this mean you are smarter for listening? And is it just Mozart? A composition by the Greek composer Yanni—whose cheesy fare you might know from infomercials—has been shown to have similar effects.

You'll have trouble finding many scientists who say Mozart makes anyone smarter. "Enjoyment arousal" is what one scientist calls it. That's certainly a good thing, but it's not enough to guarantee your children will go to Harvard—or will even prefer Mozart to their generation's version of Iron Maiden.

Q Should you wait an hour after eating to swim?

A Parents love to wheel this one out. Who hasn't been told to wait an hour after chowing down a hamburger to go back into the swimming pool?

The theory is that blood is diverted to the stomach to aid the digestive process. Since blood carries oxygen around your body, this means there's less oxygen for your muscles to utilize. This supposedly inhibits your muscles and increases the likelihood of severe muscle cramps, and could ultimately produce a rather bitter end for you at the bottom of the pool.

The math, however, doesn't add up. It takes about four hours for an average meal to fully exit your stomach, so waiting only one hour before swimming wouldn't begin to get the job done. Besides—and here's the crux of the matter—your stomach doesn't swipe enough oxygen to seriously affect your swimming; there's still plenty to go around. If you've massively pigged out before an intensive swim, you might experience muscle cramps. But if you've eaten a normal meal, it's highly unlikely.

There have been no documented cases of someone drowning because of a full stomach. The biggest risk might involve getting sick due to overexertion and sending all of that food out the way it came in. That wouldn't make your fellow swimmers particularly happy, so maybe it is best to wait an hour after eating to hop into the pool.

Q Who's more likely to give you an ulcer: your boss, your spouse, or your chef?

A So you've got a gnawing pain in your gut, huh? You can't blame it on those blazing hot Buffalo wings or on your overly demanding boss (even if he makes you come in on Saturdays). While it was once believed that stress and spicy foods were the sources of stomach ulcers, research has confirmed that nearly all ulcers are caused by bacteria.

The responsible party goes by the name *Helicobacter pylori (H. pylori)*. It can live and multiply within the protective mucus layer that covers the delicate lining of the stomach and small intestine. Most of the time, *H. pylori* just hangs out without causing any noticeable problems. But don't think that this corkscrew-shaped organism is all that innocent.

Every once in a while, *H. pylori* likes to go on a good tear. It breaks down that protective mucus layer and invades and inflames the stomach lining. As a result, you can develop an ulcer—a raw or open sore in the stomach lining. That's when the nausea, vomiting, and dull ache right above the belly button begin to set in. It might hit in the middle of the night or come and go for days or weeks at a time. But one thing's for sure: It burns like a bitch.

By now, you're probably wondering how your spouse fits into the question. Well, it's not exactly clear where *H. pylori* comes from (some suspect that it lurks in water, food, or crowded or unsanitary places). However, doctors know that the bacteria can be transmitted from person to person through close contact. That means if either you or your spouse is infected with *H. pylori,* you can pass it between the two of you through a kiss!

Regarding your boss and your chef, let's be clear that type-A personalities and zesty eating habits don't cause ulcers. However, excessive stress, alcohol, smoking, and some pain relievers can aggravate or delay the healing of existing ulcers or make you more predisposed to getting one in the first place.

Why? These irritants increase the amount of acid in your stomach, and that can help to erode the protective mucus layer—a sure invitation for any *H. pylori* in the area to wreak some havoc. The good news is that ulcers can be successfully treated with antibiotics and acid-blocking proton pump inhibitors, such as Prilosec and Nexium.

For that bit of relief, you can thank Drs. Robin Warren and Barry Marshall. In the early 1980s, these Australian pathologists were the first to suggest that bacteria were the true cause of stomach ulcers. To prove it, Marshall drank a broth of active *H. pylori* bacteria and gave himself an ulcer. For their breakthrough discovery—and self-sacrifice—the pair won the Nobel Prize in Physiology or Medicine for 2005.

Chapter Two

ORIGINS AND TRADITIONS

Q What does "kicking the bucket" have to do with death?

A Some sociologists believe that we create so many euphemisms for death because we want to avoid the subject entirely; they are used to mask our discomfort. This might explain why the phrases—including "kick the bucket"—get so colorful.

There are two possible origins of "kick the bucket," both of which are appropriately morbid. The first involves the slaughter of pigs. In days of yore, the pig was hung up by its heels from a wooden beam after its throat was slit, allowing the blood to drain out. This beam was traditionally called a "bucket," possibly because the pigs were hoisted by means of a pulley system similar to that of an old-fashioned well. In the throes of death, the pig's heels would sometimes knock against the wood. Many a butcher heard the sound of a hog kicking the "bucket."

The second possibility comes from the act of suicide by hanging. In order to do this, a person must stand upon something, secure the noose around one's neck, and either step down or kick the support away. In need of something small and easy to stand on, the theory goes, the person might choose a bucket. This expla-nation is compelling, except "kicking the bucket" doesn't refer exclusively to intentional death—the phrase is used to describe any kind of death.

Either way—whether the origin of "kicking the bucket" relates to slaughtered pigs or hangings—it isn't pretty. Of course, death is a dirty business, as evidenced by some other famous euphemisms that have been attached to it: buying the farm, pushing up daisies, taking a dirt nap, and going into the fertilizer business.

Q Why is it okay to be a daddy's girl but not a mama's boy?

A This gets right down to the heart of most human cultures: Men are supposed to be masculine, and if you're a mama's boy past the age of two or three, you're not coming across as masculine.

Psychologist Stephen Ducat put it this way in his book *The Wimp Factor: Gender Gaps, Holy Wars, and the Politics of Anxious Masculinity:* "The everyday vocabulary and common-sense notions of gender remind us that in the majority of patriarchal cultures, the most important thing about being a man is *not being a woman.*"

The restrictions aren't as great for girls, who can subordinate themselves to their fathers and still be seen as adhering to the structures and hierarchies of society. To quote Ducat again: "A daddy's little girl, on the other hand, is seen as expressing a sweet, quasi-romantic affection and idealization of her father, which often elicits a chorus of approval from friends and family."

A sociologist or anthropologist would add this layer: It is innate in animal societies for one generation to fear the generation that follows, as the rise of the younger generation coincides with the demise of the older one. This feeling is not as viciously acted out in humans as it is in wild animals, but humans are capable of far superior intellectual activity, so our treatment of this phenomenon is perhaps more nuanced.

Thus, those experts might say, a mother will align with her son because he does not represent a threat. Writes Gil A. Katz in the *International Review of Psycho-Analysis:* "It has generally been psychoanalytic wisdom, following Freud, that the first-born son, by virtue of his position as the 'undisputed darling' of his mother, the one who gives her a sense of being physically and emotionally completed, has an advantageous if not enviable lot among his siblings and is possessor of an unshakably successful outlook on life."

According to one theory, a mother can look to her son (at least in emotional terms) to support her as she grows old, but is supplanted by her daughter where a societal role is concerned. The same goes with a father and daughter: Sons usurp fathers in many ways, while daughters can continue to gratify them.

These roles are codified in society, but when a son is so attached to his mother that he doesn't assume his appropriate leadership role, he's looked upon badly. He's allowing himself to be unmanly. Or worse, to quote Shania Twain from her album *Come on Over,* he starts thinking, "Man! I feel like a woman."

Q Why do cops say you have the right to remain silent?

A It's all because of a guy named Miranda, who took his case to the United States Supreme Court.

Ernesto Miranda, who had only a grammar-school education, was arrested in 1963 for robbery and rape in his home state of Arizona. He declared his innocence, but the victim identified him. After a two-hour interrogation, Miranda signed a confession and was found guilty because of it. However, the police admitted that they hadn't told him he had the right to have an attorney present.

The Fifth Amendment to the U.S. Constitution protects Americans from having to testify against themselves. That's why people will sometimes "plead the Fifth" in court to avoid answering questions on the grounds that they may be incriminating. And the Sixth Amendment flat-out states that anyone accused of a crime has the right to "the assistance of counsel for his defense."

Miranda appealed and lost. Arizona's Supreme Court turned him down, too. But in 1966, Miranda's case was consolidated with three other similar cases from different jurisdictions and was brought before the U.S. Supreme Court. Miranda won a new trial, in which he was convicted. (He had been deprived of his constitutional rights, but that didn't mean he was innocent.)

Chief Justice Earl Warren wrote: "Prior to any questioning, the person must be warned that he has a right to remain silent, that any statement he does make may be used as evidence against him, and that he has a right to the presence of an attorney, either retained or appointed." These rights that Warren listed have been known as Miranda Rights ever since, and all law enforcement officials are required to recite them whenever they make an arrest.

In January 1976, a Phoenix police officer pulled out his small rectangular card bearing the Miranda Rights and read them to a suspect he had just arrested in a murder case. The suspect remained silent, and due to insufficient evidence was not charged in the murder. The victim? Thirty-four-year-old Ernesto Miranda, who had been stabbed to death in a Phoenix bar.

Q Why is Thanksgiving on Thursday?

A Because Abraham Lincoln said so. In his 1863 proclamation, Lincoln declared Thanksgiving to be an official national holiday. It was one way he attempted to unite the nation in the midst of the brutal Civil War. Here's what he said:

"I do therefore invite my fellow citizens in every part of the United States, and also those who are at sea and those who are sojourning in foreign lands, to set apart and observe the last Thursday of November next, as a day of Thanksgiving and Praise to our beneficent Father who dwelleth in the Heavens."

Thanksgiving was celebrated long before Honest Abe came along and gave a speech about it. According to American tradition, the Pilgrims' first Thanksgiving was observed in 1621 (it probably took place in mid-October, and no one knows for sure on which day of the week). Although the Pilgrims did not celebrate Thanksgiving the following year, over time it became a tradition for days of thanksgiving to be celebrated throughout the colonies following the fall harvest. But not all the colonies honored Thanksgiving, and not all observed is on the same day.

A unified Thanksgiving Day came about largely due to the efforts of Sarah Josepha Hale. As editor of the popular magazine *Godey's Lady Book,* Hale campaigned for a single, national day of thanksgiving for a number of years—until Lincoln granted his support in 1863. That year, Thanksgiving was celebrated on Thursday, November 26.

Why Thursday? Well, it was good enough for George Washington, who declared a one-time national day of thanksgiving on a Thursday in late November 1789. In addition, according to *The Old Farmer's Almanac,* Thursday might have become a traditional day of thanksgiving for the Puritans in order to distance the commemoration from the Sabbath day.

In 1939, President Franklin Roosevelt announced that Thanksgiving would be celebrated on the third Thursday of November instead of the last. This was an attempt to encourage earlier holiday shopping and boost the economy during the Great Depression. But not all the states complied until Congress passed a resolution in 1941 declaring that Thanksgiving would fall on the fourth Thursday of November, and that's where it remains today. Kind of makes you crave a piece of pumpkin pie, huh?

Q What's the point of the barber pole?

A Barbers date back to Egypt in the Bronze Age (circa 3500 BC). At the dawn of their profession, they were medicine men and priests. Barbers were placed at the head of their tribes and treated with utmost respect—and with good reason. A popular superstition of the time was that good and evil spirits entered and left the body through the hair. The only way to be rid of an evil spirit was to get a trim. In addition to tonsorial exorcisms, barbers baptized babies and arranged marriages.

By the Middle Ages, the barber's duties had been somewhat refined, though they were still rather broad by today's standards. On top of the usual shaves and haircuts, barbers performed minor medical procedures, such as bloodletting and pulling teeth. Bloodletting is the process of using leeches to drain blood from the body, and it was prescribed for such diverse conditions as fevers, inflammations, and even hemorrhages. The practice continued until the late nineteenth century.

The design and placement of the barber pole were inspired by bloodletting. The original wooden pole was gripped tightly by the patient, which caused his or her veins to bulge and made them easier to puncture. The poles are thought to have been painted red to mask bloodstains. Once the procedure was completed, the pole was placed outside and the linens that had been used to clean up the mess were hung on it to dry. The linens flapped in the wind and became twisted around the pole, which created the red-and-white design that is so familiar today.

The pole, with its linens flapping in the wind, served as an advertisement for the bloodletting business. The metal top of the pole, which has evolved into a spherical shape, was originally meant to signify the bowl in which the leeches were kept before a bloodletting; the bottom represented the bowl into which the leeches were placed once they were bloated with blood.

Few people today realize that the barber once held such an esteemed position in society. In contemporary society, the barbershop has been reduced to a scribble on a list of errands, somewhere to go between the hardware store and the grocery store. You might have a friendly chat with your barber while your hair is being cut, but an exorcism? That's better left to religious professionals.

Q Whose grandfather is the grandfather clock named after?

A At first blush, the answer to this question seems obvious. Think about it: When's the last time you saw a grandfather clock in the house of a person under the age of sixty? Not for some time, if ever. Grandfather clocks—with their long cases, pendulums, echoing chimes, and Roman numerals—belong to the world of parlors, davenports, rose-water perfume, angel figurines, and cut-glass bowls filled with licorice candies that have been sitting out for decades. In short, the world of grandparents.

While this may seem like the obvious answer, the real reason these timekeeping devices—technically named "longcase clocks"—picked up the grandfatherly nickname has nothing to do with grandparents. However, it has everything to do with a song that your grandparents (or more likely your great-great-grandparents) might have heard when they were young.

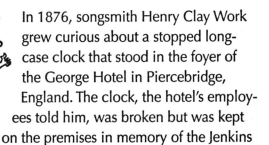

In 1876, songsmith Henry Clay Work grew curious about a stopped long-case clock that stood in the foyer of the George Hotel in Piercebridge, England. The clock, the hotel's employees told him, was broken but was kept on the premises in memory of the Jenkins brothers, two longtime proprietors of the George. Seems the clock kept perfect time throughout their lives, but when the first Jenkins brother died, it started to falter. Soon after, the second brother died and the clock stopped altogether, despite the best efforts of a host of repairmen.

Work was struck by the story (so to speak) and wrote a ditty about the clock. In the song, the timepiece is referred to as "my grand-father's clock." The first verse goes something like this:

My grandfather's clock
Was too large for the shelf,

So it stood ninety years on the floor;
It was taller by half
Than the old man himself,
Though it weighed not a pennyweight more.
It was bought on the morn
Of the day that he was born,
And was always his treasure and pride;
But it stopped short
Never to go again,
When the old man died.

Okay, perhaps old H. C. wasn't Bob Dylan. But his song was an instant hit, and soon, most people had dropped the somewhat clunky term "longcase clock" for the newer, hipper "grandfather clock."

With the advent of digital technology and atomic clocks, some clock lovers worry that the old pendulum-swinging grandfathers may not be long for the timekeeping world. However, despite its inanity, H. C. Work's song lives on. It was recorded multiple times in the twentieth century and as recently as 2004 by the R&B act Boys II Men. It's the song that keeps on ticking.

Q Why are flowers placed on graves?

A This tradition can be traced to the ancient Greeks, who performed rites over graves that were called *Zoai*. Flowers were placed on the graves of Greek warriors; it was believed that if the flowers took root and blossomed on the graves, the souls of the warriors were sending a message that they had found happiness in the next world.

The ancient Romans also used flowers to honor soldiers who died in battle. The Romans held an elaborate eight-day festival during February called *Parentalia* ("Day of the Fathers"), during which roses and violets were placed on the graves of fallen soldiers by friends and family members.

According to acclaimed historian Jay Winik, the tradition began in America at the end of the Civil War, after a train had delivered Abraham Lincoln to his final resting place in Springfield, Illinois. In his Civil War book *April 1865,* Winik writes: "Searching for some way to express their grief, countless Americans gravitated to bouquets of flowers: lilies, lilacs, roses, and orange blossoms, anything which was in bloom across the land. Thus was born a new American tradition: laying flowers at a funeral."

Following Lincoln's burial, people all over the country began decorating the graves of the more than six hundred thousand soldiers who had been killed—especially in the South, where organized women's groups also placed banners on the graves of soldiers. The practice became so widespread that in 1868, General John Alexander Logan—the leader of the Grand Army of the Republic, a Union veterans' group—issued an order designating May 30 as a day for "strewing with flowers or otherwise decorating the graves of comrades who died in defense of their country." The day was originally called Decoration Day, but it later became Memorial Day. On May 30, 1868, thousands gathered at Arlington National Cemetery in Virginia to decorate more than twenty thousand graves of Civil War soldiers. In 1873, New York became the first state to declare Decoration Day a legal holiday.

Today, the tradition is stronger than ever. In addition to being placed on graves, flowers are often displayed in funeral homes and churches for burial services. The most elaborate arrangements are positioned around the casket, perhaps hearkening back to the belief of the ancient Greeks that a flower in bloom signifies happiness in the afterlife.

Q Why can't you have your cake and eat it too?

A An excellent question! As the late comedian George Carlin said, "What good is a goddamn cake you can't eat?" But back in the fifteen hundreds, when this famous phrase came into being, folks weren't as funny (at least not purposely) and were likely trying to make a serious point.

English writer John Heywood included the original version of this saying in his 1546 book of proverbs, *A Dialogue Conteinyng the Nomber in Effect of All the Prouerbes in the Englishe Tongue*: "Wolde you bothe eate your cake, and haue your cake?" In the next century, another English poet, George Herbert, gave the phrase a more Shakespearean flair: "Wouldst thou both eat thy cake and have it?"

In both of these early versions, the eating comes before the having, which makes the phrase's meaning easier to understand. If you've snarfed down the cake, it's obviously not still on your plate, so you don't have it anymore. But after the saying made its way to the United States (first noted in 1742 in the *Colonial Records of Georgia*), its components were reversed and it began to be used in the form we know it today: "You can't have your cake and eat it, too."

This arrangement makes things a little more complex, because as Americans we are also fond of saying, "Have some cake" when we mean, "Eat some cake." The key to deciphering this sort of thing—an idiom, if you must know—is to get in touch with your most philosophical self. Linguists define an idiom as an expression whose meaning is different than the literal definition of the words involved. We're not really talking about cake here. (Idioms, not surprisingly, are one of the things about English that blows the minds of those who are trying to learn it as a second language, as well as some who are trying to learn it as a first language.)

Thinking metaphorically, then, you can't both consume something and keep it around. Things can't happen simultaneously in two contradictory ways. You have to make a choice: Are you hungry for cake now, or would you rather gaze awhile at its splendor? Because once you eat that cake, it's gone. Or, as the Rolling Stones so succinctly put it, "You can't always get what you want."

Q Why is the medical symbol a snake on a stick?

A It does seem odd, doesn't it? Most snake symbolism tends to be negative: snake oil, a snake in the grass, snake eyes, speaking with a forked tongue, and so on. But like many things that are weird and confusing, the medical symbol goes back to Greek mythology.

Asclepius was the god of medicine, but he didn't have to go to medical school to attain this status. Instead, he killed a snake and then watched as another snake with a mouthful of herbs brought the dead snake back to life. Asclepius used the same herbs to revive a man who had been killed by Zeus. From then on, Asclepius needed a catchy calling card, so naturally he took to carrying a staff with a snake on it, a symbol that is known as the asklepian.

You've probably also encountered a medical symbol with two snakes on it and some wings at the top. Where did this one come from? Like so many other things that are weird and confusing, this can be attributed to a combination of Greek mythology and ignorance. The double-snaked staff is a caduceus, the wand of Hermes, who was the Greek god of commerce. It seems that a prominent British publisher adopted the caduceus as its symbol and printed it in medical books. One influential reader of those texts—U.S. Army surgeon Captain Frederick Reynolds—mistook the caduceus for the asklepian. In 1902, Reynolds made a successful push to establish the caduceus as the official badge of Army doctors, and its misplaced usage as a medical symbol spread from there.

Depending on your opinion of doctors, this choice was either truly inspired or truly idiotic: Hermes was also the god of thieves, and in *The Odyssey,* he leads the dead to Hades.

Q Why do parties always end up in the kitchen?

A Because that's where the food comes from, friendly reader. Why wait for the tray of canapés to make its way from the kitchen through the dining room, past the great room and out onto the deck? By the time it gets to you, here's what will be left: some crumbs of Chex mix, one lousy pig in a blanket, and a teeny-tiny cucumber sandwich that doesn't really count as a sandwich anyway because it doesn't have a top or deli meat.

No, the smartest partygoers stake out a spot in the kitchen right by the range. Not so close that they feel the heat, mind you, but close enough to get first dibs on the cranberry-baked Brie at its oozing best right out of the oven.

Besides, hanging in the kitchen gives you a chance to chat it up with the hostess instead of with Larry the drill-bit salesman. In the olden days, the hostess might have been slaving away for the entirety of the party. But not anymore. Today, she's a liberated at-home chef who is surrounded by four hundred square feet of hardwood floors, travertine tiles, designer cabinet knobs, and sparkling stainless steel appliances (Sub-Zero, of course). Her kitchen is no longer a solitary workspace—it's the showpiece of her home. And she certainly doesn't mind showing it off to all her guests.

Go ahead, indulge her. Why not offer to slice a tomato or garnish the cheese ball? You can even dip your chips in the chipotle salsa without fear of dripping on the living room carpet, and sip Chardonnay from a real wine glass rather than one of those plastic two-parters with the detachable stem. You probably can even keep up with the Notre Dame game on the countertop flat-screen TV.

Best of all, being in the kitchen means that once the party hits full force, your stomach will be so full of food that the alcohol you're drinking won't get the best of you. So drink up. There's no way you'll dance with a lamp shade on your head. Leave that to Larry.

Q Why do people shake hands?

A In today's Western world, the handshake serves a number of purposes. It can be a greeting or a farewell, and it can signify congratulations or condolences. In business, a deal can be sealed with a handshake.

Where exactly did this quirky little custom originate? This question is the object of much debate, conjecture, and confusion, mainly because the handshake likely predates written history. Some historians trace the origin of the modern Western handshake—the clasping of hands—to medieval Europe. Back then, shaking hands was hardly a congenial gesture—it was more like a shakedown. Men would clasp hands to make sure that neither was concealing a weapon.

Eventually, the handshake matured into something more civilized. According to Philip A. Busterson's 1978 book *Social Rituals of the British,* writer and explorer Sir Walter Raleigh, who was noted for his manners, introduced the handshake that we know today in the late sixteenth century.

Since then, the handshake has become a nuanced custom. For instance, it's considered poor taste to greet someone with a handshake that's too strong; a limp handshake, on the other hand, is perceived as a sign of weakness. It is viewed as an insult to refuse a handshake or to fake a greeting by offering but not following through on a handshake.

Today, there are high-fives, low-fives, soul shakes, secret handshakes—you name it. The handshake's grip on civilization has tightened considerably since those days in medieval Europe, when some skin on skin meant, "I'm not going to kill you…at least not today."

Q Why do Western languages read left to right and Eastern languages right to left?

A Go ahead—ask any lefthander why we in the West read and write from left to right. We're betting that the answer will be that it's because we live in a world that's designed for the right-handed majority.

Maybe there's some truth to that. Remember how the lefty kids in your class in grade school did that awkward-looking twisty thing with their left hands while they wrote? And watch lefthanders try to write on a dry-erase board—if they aren't careful, their writing hand smudges what they've just written. There's just one fly in the ointment with that theory: Hebrew and Arabic languages, which also are written and read horizontally, go right to left. And the people who speak those languages aren't any less likely to be right-handed.

The fact is, writing systems are so old and so varied that no one can say with any certainty how they ended up the way they are. In Egyptian hieroglyphs, the direction of a line is determined by the direction the characters are facing. If the characters face left, the line is read from right to left, and vice versa.

And sometimes ancient languages were written *boustrophedon* style, meaning that the lines alternated; one line would go from right to left and then the next would go from left to right. (*Boustrophedon* is a word with Greek origins that means "to turn like oxen," as in plowing. You plow one row in one direction, and then you turn around and plow the next row in the opposite direction.) The early Greek alphabet (a direct ancestor of Western alphabets that are used today) was originally written from right to left, then *boustrophedon* style, and then eventually left to right.

Most of the major Eastern languages were influenced by Chinese. Traditional Chinese writing goes from top to bottom, with the columns progressing from right to left. Why the writing goes from top to bottom is not known, but right-handedness may have had an influence on the right-to-left progression. Early Chinese calligraphers wrote on scrolls; a right-handed calligrapher would hold a brush in the right hand while writing and use the left hand to hold and roll open the scroll. A wise left-handed calligrapher probably found another line of work.

Horizontal text has become more common in the East, particularly in China in recent years. Computer technology has contributed to this change. Ever try to write vertically with your word-processing software? You'd need the patience of a left-handed Chinese calligrapher.

Q Does it cost more to insure a red car?

A Red, the color of blood and fire, is considered to be energizing and passionate. Crimson cars, then, are known to attract all kinds of trouble, including drivers who like to push the pedal to the metal. Think the cops don't know it? A gray car and a red car are exceeding the posted speed limit. Which one is the trooper going to pull over? Thought so.

It gets worse. Speeding correlates to high-risk behavior, a factor in traffic accidents. Insurance companies track moving violations. Do you think flinty actuaries who calculate auto premiums charge more for red cars in anticipation of high collision claims? Actually, think again. When it comes to car insurance, much of what we believe about red is wrong.

Insurance companies are well aware of the red rumor. It was the number-one myth that was identified in an online survey of one thousand drivers conducted in 2005 by DriveSM, a Progressive Group auto insurance company. Of the drivers surveyed, 25 percent believed that car color affects auto insurance rates.

This notion makes underwriters see red. They assert that car color is not used to calculate auto insurance rates; instead, premiums are based on the vehicle's year, make, model, body style, and engine type. In general, the newer and more expensive the vehicle, the costlier it is to repair and, therefore, to insure. The youngest and oldest drivers pay more because they have the highest accident rates. The same holds true for men versus women, singles versus married people, and urbanites versus country folk. Miles driven plays a role, and so does your driving record, including, yes, moving violations.

If drivers of red cars do indeed behave in inordinately risky ways, America's multibillion-dollar insurance industry would probably know it. A spokesperson for State Farm Insurance, the nation's largest auto insurer with policies on forty million vehicles, notes that the legions of actuaries are highly motivated to predict risk. If they could set higher rates for red cars, they would.

Q Why do horseshoes bring luck?

A The horseshoe is like an infomercial product: It's several things rolled into one! No, the horseshoe doesn't slice and dice, but it helps to protect a horse's hoof...it's used in a game called, appropriately enough, horseshoes...and it brings good luck.

Many cultures attribute magical power to the horseshoe—such as  the ability to ward off witches, bad fairies, goblins, and other mischievous or evil creatures. So how did this utilitarian hunk of metal develop such a fine reputation?

The horseshoe's crescent shape may have a lot to do with it. From ancient moon worshippers to the Egyptians, the crescent gained a foothold as a potent symbol in mysticism and mythology. The fact that horseshoes are made from iron, which is considered a lucky metal, also has helped. Then there are the horses themselves—horses have often been regarded with reverence and awe. Occasionally, as was the case among certain Germanic tribes, horses have even been worshipped as sacred animals. With so much street cred, the horseshoe was destined to be an object of folklore and superstition.

But before you run out hunting for a horseshoe of your own, there are a few luck-related rules you need to know. First, you can't just buy a horseshoe for luck—you have to find it. Second, if there are nails still in it, that's extra lucky—but don't remove them, for gosh sakes; removing them is unlucky. And don't pick up a mule shoe—that's bad luck. The same goes for picking up a broken horseshoe—it has to be whole to be lucky. But if you find a horseshoe that came from the rear hoof of a grey mare, and it has seven nail holes instead of the standard eight, and there are still nails in it—you are totally rocking in luck, dude.

Once you locate a horseshoe, you have a few options to maximize its influence. You can spit on it and make a wish, or you can make a wish and throw it over your left shoulder. But if you aren't into the whole wish-granting thing and you'd rather just have general good luck, you can hang it over a door in your home. Depending on the school of thought you believe, it will either be essential to hang it with the curve up or the curve down. Most people hang it with the prongs up and the curve down; that way, it holds the luck like a bowl and doesn't spill it. But others feel that this keeps the luck from reaching the recipients; these folks go curve-up.

So if you find a horseshoe and you can remember these myriad rules and regulations, perhaps you'll be the luckier for it.

Q Why is a white flag a symbol of surrender?

A It seems like a cliché straight out of a 1950s B-movie or an episode of *Hogan's Heroes*. Despondent and fearing for their lives, the vanquished search desperately for anything white—a handkerchief, a shirt, a pair of underpants—and attach it to a stick. They then proceed cautiously (or, in the case of *Hogan's Heroes,* clumsily) toward their gloating foe.

In reality, the tradition of the white flag as a symbol of surrender or truce goes back a couple of thousand years. In the West, the Roman historian Tacitus mentioned a white flag of surrender that was used at the Second Battle of Cremona in AD 69. In the East, the use of a white surrender flag is believed to date back just as far.

It's unclear how the color white first came to symbolize surrender. Flag experts surmise that it happened because white is a neutral hue, one that could be easily distinguished from the colorful banners that armies often carried into battle. Today, the use of the white flag as a sign of peace or surrender is an official part of the rules of warfare, as referenced in the Geneva Conventions.

The white flag has had other military uses throughout history, though none lasted long. For a short time during the Civil War, the Confederacy used a mostly white national flag that was known as the "Stainless Banner"—however, it caused confusion in battle and was scrapped. During the sixteen hundreds, the French (those lovable contrarians) used a white flag to signify the intent to go to battle. Historians don't tell us whether the French looked with disdain at anyone who didn't understand their unconventional use of the white flag—but we can guess that they did.

Chapter Three

LOVE AND LUST

Q Do opposites attract?

A The laws of physics and energy dictate that like charges repel each other and opposite charges attract. The same can be said of human relationships. How else could the sweet girl next door end up with the biggest bastard on the block?

Dr. Paul Dobransky, author of *The Secret Psychology of How We Fall in Love,* says that when someone possesses a personality trait we lack, we naturally tend to find that person attractive. Let's say you're a little bit country and he's a little bit rock and roll—you may soon find yourself shopping for spandex pants and a new tattoo. Opposites are exciting because they add a new dimension to our lives. And that can make sparks fly. That's right—when the yin and yang are groovin', everything's feeling pretty good.

What if you are an anal-retentive clean freak and he leaves dirty dishes in the sink? At first, it's kind of endearing. But after a few months of "appreciating" each other's disparities, the honeymoon ends. Eventually you discover that he's a practicing Wiccan who drinks three Red Bulls a day and doesn't pay bills on time. And if he leaves one more fricking piece of Fiestaware in the sink, you're going to smash it over his mullet-topped head.

That's not to say opposites who attract can't make it work. "A shy person plus an outgoing person are a great match when they agree on politics, religion, and life goals," Dobransky says. There's the kicker. Sometimes, opposites fit like puzzle pieces: Combine the best attributes and worst flaws of each, and somehow you get the makings of one complete person. However, when you throw polarizing personal views and values into the mix—we're talking money, education, children, and Yankees versus Red Sox—you have a recipe for disaster.

Dr. Neil Clark Warren, a clinical psychologist and the author of *Date…or Soul Mate? How to Know if Someone is Worth Pursuing in Two Dates or Less,* says opposites often attract, but they can drive each other crazy over the long haul. His advice? Find someone similar to you. "When two people come from similar backgrounds, they operate from a position of strength," Warren says. "Their relationship is made significantly easier by all the customs and practices they have in common."

So skip the stress and strain of ceiling fan on or ceiling fan off, stay in or go out, Lexis hybrid or Harley Fat Boy. Want to be happy?

Take a look in the mirror and find someone who's quite literally a reflection of you.

Q Do nerds make better lovers?

A While diligently researching this probing question, we were shocked to discover how much media attention it has received. Here at F.Y.I. headquarters, we can only speculate about those who would sift through the mountains of accumulated information on the subject. Are they from the legion of nerds, grasping at justification for their nerdy lifestyle? Are they regular folk who are considering defecting to the geek team in an attempt to become better lovers?

Our conclusion: If you're turning to a magazine, newspaper, or Internet article to gauge your sexual prowess, you probably suck in bed. Let's peek under the covers.

The articles we mined fell into two categories. We'll call the first "Nerd Makes Good." These articles describe how various dweebs have been able to land mega-hot babes who should be out of their leagues. For instance, an article from 2005 in the New York *Daily News* details how pairings such as Marilyn Monroe and Arthur Miller and Christina Aguilera and music exec Jordan Bratman prove that nerds can score some primo tail despite not being classi-

cally cool. It must be observed, however, that these articles tend to describe how dorks can be stable, compassionate breadwinners—noticeably absent is any discussion of the boudoir.

We'll call the second category "Geek Is Good." Articles under this banner take the negative trappings of nerddom and spin them into positives. Predictably, these articles are written by geeks, for geeks. Take a story from a 2007 issue of the dork bible *Wired,* titled "The 10 Real Reasons Why Geeks Make Better Lovers." Look no further than the article's second entry, "Geeks dig consensual role playing," to conclude that "better lover" in geek-speak must mean "terrible lay." The problem is that the author is thinking too hard. Having sex isn't some theorem that can be proved with a numbered list—it's supposed to be about passion and spontaneity.

What's sorely missing from these puff pieces is common sense. It comes down to practice, gentle reader. Think the first time you pick up a cello you're going to start sawing away like Yo-Yo Ma? Of course not! Are nerds better lovers? No way. They're too busy memorizing the periodic table or gluing felt crescent moons onto their conical wizard hats to find their way into the sack.

Q Can men have multiple orgasms?

A Men and women are set up differently when it comes to sex. A woman's orgasm has nothing to do with the completion of her fundamental reproductive task: receiving sperm in order to fertilize her egg. She can enjoy orgasms till the cows come home without affecting her ability to receive seminal fluid. For a man, sex is inherently about providing semen—and once the job is done, he is too. Or is he?

For thousands of years, male Taoists, as well as men who practice Tantric sex, have been able to achieve multiple orgasms by using what's called the "finger-locking technique." This method involves applying pressure to the perineum, or "taint" (the soft spot just between the anus and the scrotum), so that semen does not travel out but circulates back into the body. Taoist teachers refer to the perineum as the "million-dollar point."

Here's how the method works, men: If you cross the tips of your ring and middle fingers over your index finger, you will create a small triangle. Just before you reach "ejaculatory inevitability"— which is when you know that one more stroke of the hand or hip thrust will put you over the top—place the tip of your index finger onto the urethra, just in front of the anus, via the perineum.

Taoist and Tantrics believe that when you expel your semen, you not only deplete your body of four meals worth of protein, vitamins, and minerals, but you also diminish your *chi*. Food, we all know, is easy to come by, but not so with *chi*. *Chi* isn't something you can just pick up at your local fast-food joint or supermarket. It flows throughout your body in the form of energy—think of it as your body's electromagnetic force. When your *chi* is surging powerfully and uninterrupted, your body is at its optimal level of performance; when your *chi* is weak, your body becomes sick and ineffectual.

Taoists believe that the finger-locking technique enables you to channel all of that orgasmic energy up your spinal cord and through your seven *chakras* (energy centers), culminating in a mind-blowing sensatory experience. Due to electromagnetic stimulation, you will not experience any drowsiness post-orgasm. And, of course, you'll be ready to go again.

Q If diamonds are forever, why do so many couples get divorced?

A The mind boggles at the potential snappy answers to this silly question. A diamond is not the source of strength in marriage; it is merely an expensive metaphor for hoped-for permanence. Anyone who depends on a diamond to keep a marriage alive would do better to watch Dr. Phil; at least that's free.

There is no cause-and-effect relationship between diamonds, which symbolize strength in marriage, and strong marriages. Nothing that occurs naturally on the planet is stronger than the diamond, which is made of carbon atoms that are bonded within the earth under great heat and pressure. Ancient people knew the strength of diamonds—the Greeks called a diamond *adamas*, which means "invincible."

The use of diamonds in rings traces back at least to the Romans, who felt the gemstone had magic powers, such as the abilities to counteract poison, prevent insanity, and offset anxieties. (Insert your marriage joke here.) It wasn't until the 1930s, however, that diamonds became inexorably linked to a romantic ideal. To boost sagging sales, the De Beers diamond company launched an advertising campaign that romanticized diamonds. Then, in 1948, the De Beers ad team created the tag line "A Diamond Is Forever"— and the gem became synonymous with marriage.

Marriage hasn't been as durable as the De Beers slogan. According to data from the U.S. Census Bureau, roughly 80 percent of first marriages in the 1950s lasted at least fifteen years; among people who married for the first time in the late 1980s, about 60 percent made it to the fifteen-year mark.

But just as marriage has come under attack by the forces of modern life, so has the diamond and its designation as the hardest material on the planet. At least four synthetic substances now are harder than diamonds (hardness being measured by scratch-resistance): borazon, ultrahard fullerite, rhenium diboride, and aggregated diamond nanorods. These substances have use in manufacturing and other processes, but why haven't they been pressed into service as symbols of marriage?

Q Would men still live in caves if it weren't for women?

A It's true: We've got women to thank for many of the greatest innovations of the modern age. We're talking about things like dishwashers (Josephine Cochran), windshield wipers (Mary Anderson), disposable diapers (Marion Donovan), liquid paper (Bette Nesmith Graham), the first computer language (Grace Murray Hopper), and Kevlar (Stephanie Kwolek), a synthetic material that's five times as strong as steel.

Researchers are now saying that women have always been major players in society. In their book *The Invisible Sex: Uncovering the True Roles of Women in Prehistory,* archaeologist J. M. Adovasio, anthropologist Olga Soffer, and writer Jake Page assert that early women drove the invention of language, agriculture, and the most useful tools, particularly string. They call it the String Revolution, and it opened the door to weaving the first clothes, baskets, food containers, and slings, as well as nets to catch game and fish for food. Talk about advancing humankind! If women were the primary weavers and fabric experts of prehistory, it's no wonder that they're still so good at decorating—and redecorating—with draperies, bed linens, and shabby-chic pillowcases. And it's probably no coincidence that the inventor of the Scotchgard line of stain repellents and cleaners was a woman (Patsy Sherman)—the ladies do like to keep their woven upholstery and carpets clean.

Yes, of the two sexes, it's the women who really know how to turn houses into comfy, cozy homes, complete with complementary color schemes and furnishings. Left to their own devices, most men would be content living in a tent or a cave—so long as those domiciles are equipped with a beat-up Barcalounger, mini-fridge, and cable television with a remote control.

Maybe that's why some men still do live in caves. That's right—in places like northern China, southern Spain, and Tunisia, people continue to occupy natural mountain grottos and stone caves.

Some of these earth dwellings have been outfitted with modern conveniences like electricity, running water, broadband connections, and Jacuzzis. And okay, some women live there, too.

Thanks to them, the guys have finally advanced beyond communicating with grunts and groans.

Q Why did women start wearing makeup?

A Today, most women—and some men—apply makeup for one simple reason: They want to look good. Those subtle touches of pigment and shade can make all the difference, hiding flaws in the skin and enhancing the natural appearance of facial features. Call it vanity, if you must, but spending quality time in front of a mirror is a daily ritual that millions of Americans can't do without, whether they're preparing for an average day at work, a big event, or a date with that special someone.

It all goes back to the ancient Egyptians, who were the first people to wear makeup. In a way, their basic motive was the same—just like modern day supermodels, the well-to-do women of ancient Egypt wanted to look their best and saw the careful application of face-paint as the means to that end.

But they weren't just trying to impress a burly construction fore-man who was working on the pyramids or a distinguished assistant to Pharaoh. Their sights were set a little higher—they were trying to impress the gods. Archeological evidence shows that Egyptians were dolling themselves up as early as 4000 BC, in part because they felt that their appearance was directly related to their spiritual worth.

So the Egyptians created the first cosmetics. (No word on whether they received makeovers at malls along the Nile.) They applied an eye paint called mesdemet (from the ancient Egyptian word *msdmt*), a mixture of copper and lead ore, around their eyes. Green shades went on the lower eyelids; black and dark gray were applied to the lashes and upper eyelids. Dark colors were said to ward off "evil eyes." To complete the ornate look around the eyes, they added almond shapes of a dark-colored powder (later called kohl) that might have been a combination of ingredients such as burnt almonds, oxidized copper, copper ores, lead, ash, and ochre. (Think Johnny Depp as Captain Jack Sparrow or Keith Richards as Keith Richards.) Kohl was believed to have medicinal benefits as well.

Egyptian women put a mixture of red clay or ochre and water or animal fat on their cheeks and lips—the first blush and lipstick—and applied henna to their nails. When it came to removing all of these cosmetics at the end of the day, they used a type of soap made from vegetable and animal oils and perfumes.

The connection between beauty and spirituality remained for centuries, until the Romans gained power. The Romans adopted many of the Egyptians' cosmetic formulas, but their primary motive was to improve their appearance for each other and not the gods. Even back then, it would seem, hotties turned heads.

Q Why do we call homosexuals "gay"?

A Long before the word "gay" had any connection to homosexuals, it meant "full of joy" or "brilliant and gaudy" (as in how a person was dressed). The word wasn't used to describe homosexuals until the late eighteen hundreds.

Around the turn of the twentieth century, hobos traveled the continental United States via train cars, panhandling and providing menial tasks in return for spare change. A boy who was a traveling companion of and an apprentice to a hobo was referred to as a "gey cat." When panhandling didn't get the job done, the young hobos would provide sexual favors to strangers of either gender in exchange for money. Furthermore, the nature of a gey cat's status as an apprentice was catamite, meaning that he provided sex to the older hobos in return for being taught the vagabonding ropes.

Homosexual men called each other "gay" by the 1920s, and the term made its theatrical debut in 1929 in Noel Coward's operetta *Bitter Sweet* in the lyrics of the song "Green Carnation." The song alluded to Oscar Wilde, who was famously homosexual and always wore a green carnation. (In Wilde's Paris of the late nineteenth century, it was fashionable for a gay man to wear a green carnation in his lapel hole.)

Hollywood latched on to the trendy meaning of the word and brought it to a national audience in 1938. In the movie *Bringing Up Baby*, Cary Grant's character is portrayed as effeminate, while his leading lady, Katherine Hepburn, is the overpowering and demanding one. The role reversal wasn't something that audiences of the era were used to seeing. In one scene, Grant's character has to wear women's clothing and says that he "just went gay, all of a sudden!"

"Gay" soon became an accepted antonym for heterosexual; it was the least offensive word that was available at the time. In fact, calling someone a "homosexual" was a slur of sorts. Up until 1973, homosexuality was listed as a clinically diagnosed mental illness in the *Diagnostic and Statistical Manual of Mental Disorders*. "Queer," another common way to describe a homosexual person, means "odd" and has derogatory undertones.

Although today the word "gay" can also mean "lame" and "boring," thanks to the youth of the late 1990s, it is most widely used in the context of homosexuality. "Gay" is considered a politically correct way to describe homosexuals, but it can be offensive if misused. Here's an example: Acceptable: "Those gay men in the bar were rather stylishly dressed." Offensive: "Did you see the way those gay guys were dressed?"

The bottom line? Even though it's common, "gay" is not a word to be bandied about carelessly.

Q Why is a romantic holiday named after Saint Valentine?

A Love and war hardly seem to mix well, but in the case of Saint Valentine's Day, it took war to make love. Or at least a lovers' holiday.

Valentine was a priest and physician in Rome during the reign of Claudius the Goth in the third century AD. Claudius, who was at war with many different nations, considered how best to attract soldiers to serve him. Thinking that single men were more likely to enlist, Claudius declared that young men were forbidden to marry for one year.

Valentine, who was sympathetic to young lovers kept apart by this decree, performed weddings in secret. He was most likely also doing some other anti-Roman things, such as helping Christians break out of prison and hiding believers. Valentine eventually landed in prison and was beheaded on February 14, 269 or 270.

According to legend, Valentine continued to marry couples while he was in prison and even restored the sight of the jailer's blind daughter. The legend claims that Valentine sent her a farewell note the night before he was executed, signing it, "From your Valentine." Not only was he a friend to lovers who were kept apart by Claudius's decree, but he also made the first Valentine card.

According to noted eighteenth-century religious historian Alban Butler, Saint Valentine might not have become so famous if the Romans hadn't celebrated the holiday Lupercalia on February 15, the day after the anniversary of Valentine's martyrdom. Also known as Februata Juno (celebrating Juno, the goddess of marriage), Lupercalia began with the sacrifice of a goat. The goat's flesh was cut into strips, which young Roman men used to swat young women to promote fertility. Then a drawing took place in which unmarried men and women were paired to be lovers for the duration of the festival or for as long as a year. Lupercalia was a celebration of love, but not of the chaste and pious love that early Christians wanted to encourage.

When the Roman emperor Constantine converted to Christianity in 313 and ended the persecution of Christians with the Edict of Milan, church leaders replaced pagan rituals and holidays with Christian celebrations and commemorations. Pope Galasius declared February 14 to be Saint Valentine's Day, and the Lupercalia holiday was abandoned. According to Butler, priests encouraged the young people in their congregations to celebrate Valentine's Day with feasts, masses in Valentine's honor, and engagement announcements.

Cards, gifts, flowers, and poetry about romantic love didn't become part of the Valentine's Day tradition until much later. In

1969, Saint Valentine's Day was dropped from the official Catholic calendar of saint days because so little information is known about its namesake. Valentine remains a saint, but without an "official" day. Nevertheless, he is celebrated everywhere by people who are in love with this simple declaration: "From your Valentine."

Chapter Four

ANIMAL KINGDOM

Q Do migrating birds ever get lost?

A That depends on what you mean by "lost." Migrating birds sometimes stray from their usual course due to powerful winds and harsh weather, so they might end up thousands of miles from their intended destination. But even then, the migrating bird is never truly disoriented. Birds are known to traverse oceans by accident or swap continents without ever planning to do so, but often these misdirected travelers return to their original nesting grounds the following year. Such is the go-with-the-flow lifestyle of our feathered friends: A gust of wind in the wrong direction and they're spending the winter on West Africa's Gold Coast instead of in the Florida Keys. No biggie.

But how do migrating birds always know where they are, even when they're in the wrong place? They use visual cues, along with the mysterious force of geomagnetism, to chart their travel.

During the day, birds can look at the movement of the sun to ascertain their position. Homing pigeons, for example, use the sun as a compass. In an experiment in which homing pigeons were exposed to an artificial, twenty-four-hour light, the birds lost track of the sun's location. Upon their release, they were unable to navigate properly.

Night-flying birds use the stars to orient themselves; like sailors of old, they use the position of the North Star as a guide. This form of visual navigation has also been verified by a scientific experiment. Two sets of birds were kept in a planetarium. One set was shown constellations revolving around the North Star, as per usual; the second set was shown constellations revolving around Betelgeuse (a different star). Upon release, the first set was able to orient itself properly, but the second was not.

There are other, more down-to-earth sights that help birds plot a trip. It is common to see birds following a coastline, the meandering path of a river, or the course of a mountain range.

When visual aids fail, migrating birds have another tool at their disposal: geomagnetism. Many animals in addition to birds—salmon and bats, for example—have small amounts of magnetite inside their heads. This element reacts to changes in the earth's magnetic field and gives the animal an innate sense of direction, much as the fluctuation of fluid in our inner ears gives us an innate sense of balance. Some scientists believe that birds even use their sense of smell to enhance their mental maps.

But how do birds decide where they want to go in the first place? Some scientists believe it comes down to hereditary memory, which would inform a youngster of the route it must take to join the rest of its species at breeding time. There are enough examples of abandoned young making such journeys for this explanation to seem plausible. For example, many species of birds do not bring their offspring along when they migrate; they leave them to find their own way.

Can you blame them? Round trips for some birds can be as long as twenty-five thousand miles. Imagine the little birds continually chirping, "Are we there yet?" As humans know, it would be enough to drive the big birds crazy.

Q Is cheese really a mouse's favorite food?

A Who moved your cheese? Chances are, if you are a mouse, you won't care all that much. But relocating your peanut butter, corn chips, or chocolate? That's another matter entirely.

We've all seen the cute cartoons of mice nibbling away on a big, luscious hunk of cheese. In 2006, however, Dr. David Holmes, an animal behaviorist at Britain's Manchester Metropolitan University, stunned the world when he announced: No, mice really don't like cheese.

"Mice Hate Cheese!" the venerable *Manchester Guardian* declared. Other news sources mourned the break-up of the old "mice–cheese love team." Not surprisingly, Holmes and his colleagues were bombarded with messages from irate cooks, telling them that mice certainly do eat cheese, along with fried chicken, salami sandwiches, and anything else they can get their thieving paws on, including the plastic coating that insulates copper wires. (Mice have been to blame for more than one short circuit in the kitchen.)

To defuse the tense situation, Holmes explained that his research was intended to identify those foods preferred by a wide range of animals under optimal conditions. Yes, mice eat many things, he stated, but they evolved as vegetarians. That means their ideal meal consists of grains, nuts, seeds, beans, fruits, and other substances high in carbohydrates and sugar—which explains the little rodents' predilection for chocolate.

Where did the myth that mice love cheese come from? No one knows, exactly. One thought is that mice were known to be stowaways on ships, hiding themselves in the holes of Swiss cheese. When sailors found mice in the cheese, they that assumed it was because mice loved cheese.

Before refrigeration, cheese was stored in the pantry. Because making cheese is a labor-intensive process and uses a lot of precious milk, people were probably angrier then usual when they discovered that they were sharing their cheddar with furry invaders. Or perhaps the old folktale about the city mouse that impressed its country cousin with a gourmet spread of cosmopolitan treats created the impression that mice like rich, fatty foods.

In reality, researchers discovered that high concentrations of fat can give mice indigestion, which puts cheese fairly far down on their list of preferred snacks. So you can keep your Brie, Stilton, and Camembert. If you really want to catch a mouse, try a dab of peanut butter, a piece of potato, or a few raisins—the chocolate-covered kind should do nicely.

Q Why do mosquitoes bite some people more than others?

A Mosquitoes are attracted to some people for the same reason that some folks are attracted to bakeries early in the morning: The goods smell delicious.

One theory suggests that mosquitoes are picky eaters that choose potential victims based on blood type. Eighty-five percent of humans secrete a chemical marker through their pores that indicates their blood type. In some cases, the marker hits the mosquito the same way the smell of fresh-baked bread hits human nostrils. Microscopic drops of saliva form around the insect's proboscis, the little devil hits the smorgasbord, and it digs in as soon as it feels safe.

A study conducted in 2004 showed that mosquitoes land on individuals with Type O blood more often than they feast on those with any other blood type. Conversely, Type A appears to be the least popular flavor for mosquitoes. The fortunate 15 percent of humanity whose pores do not secrete a blood-type marker suffer the fewest bites; like a roadside diner with a burned-out neon sign, they attract hardly any customers at all.

In 2006, scientists performed a test using a Y-shaped tube. Two individuals stuck a hand in the tube, and mosquitoes that were released into the tube could choose which hand to bite. Scientists collected perspiration from the person who attracted the fewest mosquitoes to study its chemical makeup. Researchers also believe that some people may emit a masking odor that actually repels mosquitoes. By studying the chemicals these lucky people excrete, scientists hope to create a more potent, less irritating insect repellent.

Pregnant women might be particularly interested in such a breakthrough. Mosquitoes are attracted to carbon dioxide, and pregnant women exhale more carbon dioxide than the average person. Furthermore, a pregnant belly is a bit warmer than a normal belly, which may also appeal to mosquitoes.

Alcohol consumption has also been shown to increase the likelihood of bites. This may be because of a change in the blood's chemical make-up when it is processing a few drinks, and because of the rise in body temperature that comes with getting a buzz on.

Want to avoid mosquito bites? Stay away from alcohol, don't go outside if you are pregnant, and pray that you are among the lucky 15 percent of the population that doesn't secrete blood-type markers. If nothing else, hope others in your party have their neon lights flashing "Type O!"

Q Can fish walk?

A It's hard being a big fish in a small pond. When food gets scarce, there's no place to go. Unless, of course, you are a *Clarias batrachus, Anabas testudineus,* or *Periophthalmus modestus.* In that case, you just climb onto dry land and go looking for new digs.

The walking catfish, climbing gourami, and mudskipper, as they are respectively commonly known, are the three main species of ambulatory fish—fish that leave the water voluntarily rather than at the end of a line.

The walking catfish, which can grow to be nearly a foot long, has an omnivorous appetite and a nasty sting, and is the most notorious of the bunch. Native to southeast Asia, it is also found in Sri Lanka, eastern India, and the Philippines. It arrived in the United States in the early 1960s as an aquarium fish that was imported to southern Florida by exotic animal dealers. A few escaped into the wild, and by the  1970s they had spread to freshwater ponds throughout the state.

In reality, "walking" is not quite how this catfish gets around. The Thai call it the "dull-colored wriggling fish," a far more accurate description. On land, the catfish propels itself along with a snake-like motion. It breathes though labyrinth organs, which are located above the gills and absorb oxygen from the air. How far can these creatures walk (or wriggle)? A few yards at the most, according to observers.

The climbing gourami, another freshwater denizen, does the walking catfish one better. Originally from Africa, these fish can now be found in India, Malaysia, southeast Asia, and the Philippines. The gourami uses its gill plates, fins, and tail as primitive legs, and has been reported to climb over small trees on its journeys from pond to pond. Like the walking catfish, the gourami breathes through labyrinth organs and can survive for several hours on land, as long as its skin remains moist.

The third member of this trio, the mudskipper, is the champ among walking fish. It is the most widespread, too, found on the coasts of west Africa, Australia, Madagascar, India, Japan, Indonesia, and the Philippines. Genuinely amphibious, the mudskipper seems just as comfortable on land as in the water. These fish venture ashore for extended periods of time, using their strong pectoral fins and tail for locomotion. They can even flip themselves like acrobats. Oxygen is absorbed directly through the mudskippers' skin by a process known as cutaneous air breathing. In fact, the mudskipper is so well adapted to land, it will drown if it spends too much time submerged in the water without a trip to the surface for a breath of fresh air.

So if you happen to see a walking fish on your next tropical vacation, it's not because you had a few too many Mai Tais. That fish is probably out taking a stroll when the tide is low. Just like you.

Q Why do cats have nine lives?

A Okay, a cat doesn't really have nine lives—as far as we know, anyway—but it has always been considered a particularly hardy, tenacious, and resilient animal.

Cats were worshipped in ancient Egypt, where the "nine lives" thing may have gotten its legs. In the city of On, priests worshipped Atum-Ra, a sun god who gave life to the gods of air, water, earth, and sky, who in turn created the gods Osiris, Isis, Seth, and Nephthys. Collectively, these gods were called the *Ennead*—"the Nine." Atum-Ra, who embodied all nine gods (including himself), took the form of a cat when he visited the underworld. So the number nine may have historically come to be associated with cats.

Do cats have an ability to outsmart death? Absolutely, especially when they fall great distances. As a cat plummets, it reaches a nonfatal terminal falling velocity—the friction between itself and the air reduces the acceleration rate to zero. Then, the cat instinctively twists around so that it presents its stomach and becomes like a parachute, with its paws positioned so that it can land on all fours.

In medieval Europe, cats had ample opportunities to test their landing techniques. Unlike in ancient Egypt, cats were treated miserably; during a siege, diseased cats were sometimes thrown over castle walls in hopes that they would infect foes.

The Belgium town of Ypres is famous for its Cloth Hall, which was built in the early 1300s to house a thriving textile trade. Cats killed the rats that were destroying the fabric stored in Cloth Hall. But for reasons that may have to do with felines being linked to witchcraft during the era, cats were heaved once a year from the Cloth Hall tower. In modern times, Ypres has turned this long-ago event into an opportunity for tourism. Once every three years, the town hosts a cat festival in which toy cats are chucked from the towers.

Why not use real cats? They would most likely survive. Or at worst, simply use up one of their nine lives.

Q Is glue made from old horses?

A Sometimes. You may have seen it in an old movie or a vintage cartoon: A horse behaves badly or gets old, and its owner threatens it with a trip to the glue factory. And at one time, the glue factory really was a common destination for old or unwanted horses.

For hundreds of years, glue was made from collagen, a protein found in abundance in the cartilage, bones, hooves, and connective tissues of horses and other animals. Boiling these tissues for a long time breaks them down into gelatin, which can be used in everything from food products to, yes, glue.

In the decades following the Industrial Revolution in the late eighteenth century, improvements in manufacturing and chemical processes resulted in glues that were made from synthetic materials, such as plastic. Synthetic glues are often stronger than those that are made from animal products, and they hold up better under a variety of conditions. They are often easier to use, too, since many animal-derived glues are dry and must be heated and maintained at specific temperatures to remain in liquid form. Glues from animal products can also grow molds and bacteria over time, and they tend to smell bad.

There are, however, a few animal-derived glues that are still on the market. These are usually made from beef or pork by-products, but some can contain horse, too. Hide glue, for example, might be made from the hides of horses or cows. Craftsmen such as violin makers or repairers prefer hide glue because violins need to be periodically disassembled for maintenance. Pieces that are bonded with hide glue can be taken apart and re-glued more easily than those adhered with synthetic glues, which ensures that the violin's appearance and function aren't marred. Hide glue also is popular with furniture repairers.

So while you can still find certain glues that are made from horses, the stuff you use around your house is more likely to be Elmer's than Trigger's.

Q How do shellfish have sex?

A They don't have any happening nightclubs, Viagra, stiff drinks, or cheesy pickup lines. But that doesn't mean shellfish aren't getting lucky. Oysters, mussels, clams, crabs, lobsters, shrimp, and thousands of other varieties of shellfish have their own unique mating techniques, some of which just might make you blush.

Take lobsters. When the female is ready for action, she releases a pheromone—a chemical that has the effect of a sexy perfume—into the den of the male she desires. He comes out of his bachelor pad aggressively and then returns to it with his new girlfriend. Eventually, the female molts, or sheds her hard shell, and the male gently turns her over for mating. The female stays in the male's den for about a week until her new shell hardens. (No word on whether he ever calls again.)

Crabs have a similar ritual; the female also molts before mating. However, this is preceded by a scene reminiscent of a frat party.

The male tries to impress the female by standing on the tips of his walking legs and rocking from side to side. (Researchers have yet to determine whether he's wearing a toga.) Even if the female likes what she sees and accepts the invitation, she still plays hard to get for a bit. The male carries the female around for a few days before she molts. They then mate—brace yourself—for a few hours. When they are finished, the male cradles the female until her new shell hardens. (Who says all men are pigs?)

As with crabs and lobsters, shrimp mate just after the female molts. When it comes to going for a roll in the seaweed, shrimp appear to be creatures of habit—not unlike some human couples, shrimp generally mate three times a year (in the spring, summer, and winter).

The mating habits of mussels, clams, and oysters are downright wacky. With all three varieties, an adult male shoots sperm into the water. The target is, of course, a female, who is holding thousands of eggs in her gills. She catches all the sperm she can and then begins fertilization.

As this sexual sampling proves, shellfish might look like they're just sitting around, but that's hardly the case. Being encumbered by a shell hasn't stopped them from swinging.

Q Why do people dress up their pets?

A People dress up their pets for several reasons, some practical and some psychological.

On the practical side, certain breeds of dogs don't have enough meat on their bones or fur in their coats to keep themselves warm  in cold weather, so you can buy little coats or wraps to help them stay warm. Of course, you can also buy your dog a bathing suit, though there's no physiological need for it. Indeed, Web sites sell thousands of doggie Halloween costumes, from pirates to princesses, Superman to Darth Vader. Yes, we humans find animals cute, and some of us find them even cuter when they are dressed to the nines.

And this brings us to the psychological part of the equation. Many people consider a pet a member of the family; some folks even treat their pets as equals. Perhaps that helps explain why Americans in 2008 spent in the neighborhood of forty-three billion dollars on their dogs, cats, horses, hamsters, rabbits, and occasionally squirrels.

Why else might we be putting capes on our dogs or Santa hats on our cats? One study suggests it may be because we are lonely. In a study conducted at the University of Chicago, ninety-nine people were asked to describe their own pet or a pet of someone they knew. The lonelier the people were in their everyday lives, the more likely they were to use human traits to describe the pets, employing such words as "thoughtful" and "sympathetic."

We are social creatures. When the need to connect with other humans is not fulfilled, we find ways to fill the void. For some, Mr. Fluffy in a woolly sweater fits the bill.

Q How do we know that elephants never forget?

A Elephants would be excellent in the business world. Working elephants in Myanmar have been shown to remember verbal commands, other animals, and people. Considering the way they store memories of their interactions, elephants appear biologically disposed to networking. An elephant never draws a blank, leading to a famous saying: "An elephant never forgets."

Studies have revealed that as an elephant ages, its memory improves. When approached by an outsider, a matriarch often signals to the rest of the herd whether the stranger is a friend or a foe. She uses her personal experiences, as well as her sense of smell and contact cues, to protect her brood from rogue and possibly violent bull elephants. The matriarch passes her knowledge on to other members of her herd. (This was determined from a study of twenty-one elephant families during a seven-year period in Kenya.)

The same survival instinct comes into play when an elephant smells a member of a familiar group that is known to kill elephants. When an elephant catches a whiff of one of these hunters, it will race for safety. If the elephant smells a member of a group that is known to not kill elephants, it will continue grazing in the area. The elephant remembers scents, and it can differentiate between one that means danger and one that doesn't.

The saying itself is likely an alteration of an old Greek proverb: "A camel never forgets an injury." Camels were swapped out for elephants early in the twentieth century, after intelligence and an impressive capacity for recall were observed in the latter. It has become common to say someone has an "elephantine" memory—

which is much more acceptable than saying that someone has an elephantine body.

Q Why do dogs get their own years?

A Everyone knows the dog-year formula: One human year equals seven dog years. But the truth is, the dog-year formula adds up to a pile of dog doo-doo.

Why does a dog-year formula even exist? Well, it's only natural that we would want to relate to our canines in human ways, and this includes their age. With the average American man living into the mid-seventies and the average women living to seventy-nine, it's hard to look at our eleven-year-old Great Dane and think he is geriatric.

Hence, the dog-year formula. It is not known exactly why or how the seven-to-one equation became so popular—we suspect the masses latched on to its sheer simplicity and never let go—but we can easily point out its fatal flaw: Dogs become capable of reproducing around their first birthday. If you know a seven-year-old child who can do that, put down this book and call your local news station because you just became the lead story. Right there, the sacred seven-to-one theory becomes hooey.

The first year of a dog's life is similar to a human's first fifteen years. And at the end of its second year, a dog is approximately twenty-four in human years. After that, each human year is in the neighborhood of four years for Rover. If Rover makes it to the ripe old age of fifteen, he will be roughly seventy-six in human years.

However, even this formula, while much more accurate than the seven-to-one equation, is by no means foolproof. Unlike with humans, who are relatively uniform as a species, there are a number of variables that create great discrepancies between how long different types of dogs live. Size is one major factor—small dogs generally live longer than large ones. Breed is another—for example, terriers can live more than 40 percent longer than bloodhounds (up to sixteen years versus nine to eleven years).

But just like that uncle who smoked too many cigars and drank too much whiskey yet lived to be ninety-three, dogs sometimes defy the odds. Take Bluey, an Australian cattle dog who lived twenty-nine years before shuffling off his mortal coil in 1939. This is thought to be the canine longevity record. In case you're wondering, Bluey made it to about 129 in human years—which is older than dirt by any measure.

Q Why do roosters crow at sunrise?

A It's an image of bucolic splendor that we've all seen on TV and in the movies: A proud, majestic rooster, perched on an old wooden fence and silhouetted by the rising sun, lets out a familiar sound that signals the start of yet another glorious day. *Cock-a-doodle-doo!* Ah, the simple pleasures of country life.

Of course, if you have no reason to be awakened at the crack of dawn, the sound of a shrieking, crap-eating little beast loses its pastoral appeal in a big hurry. What causes this annoying behavior, anyway?

Most birds, roosters included, participate in what is known as the "dawn chorus." Because they are driven by circadian rhythms (that's what we lay folk refer to as the "body clock"), they start their day obscenely early—at or near sunrise—and their first task is to sing out. Roosters do this for a couple of reasons: to establish their territory and as a mating call. Sometimes they crow from a higher vantage point so that their call will travel farther.

A rooster's crow, then, is simply its contribution to the dawn chorus—albeit an unusually loud and obnoxious contribution.

Q Why do monkeys have red butts?

A They're better for sitting. And for attracting a mate. And for preventing their owners from getting lost in the jungle. Those red butts have a lot of tasks assigned to them.

Rosy butt pads can be found exclusively on Old World monkeys, such as baboons and mandrills, that come from Africa and Asia. These species aren't to be confused with the smaller, long-tailed New World monkeys that live in Central and South America—no red butts on those critters. (Evidently, their lighter weights and ability to swing through the trees on prehensile tails have allowed them to get by without flamboyant backsides.)

Known as ischial callosities, these thick, padded backsides make it much more comfortable for monkeys to sit on whatever rock, patch of packed dirt, or tree branch they find. This is particularly important because sitting is the Old World monkey's preferred stance for feeding and sleeping (two activities that consume a great portion of the average monkey's day).

For some monkeys, these butt pads are a drab shade of gray; other species have pinkish bums. This can help groups of monkeys make their way through the jungle or forest, since their colorful rears serve the same purpose as matching T-shirts for a family at the state fair. Don't want to get lost? Keep your eyes on the red butt ahead.

Mating is another essential monkey activity, and when females are in heat, an area of skin near their butt pads helps signal to males that the time is right for some jungle love. During these times of excitement, this area swells tremendously, obscuring the butt pads and turning a vivid shade of red or pink. The males see this helpful, non-subtle sign and know just what to do.

And in case you're wondering, Old World monkeys are the family most closely related to apes and, therefore, humans. Perhaps this helps explain our own species' primal interest in what we affectionately call "booty."

Q If an animal is stressed before being slaughtered, will it taste worse?

A Let's say you're driving down the highway and you see one of those trucks full of cattle. There are certain people (you know who you are) with a personality trait—let's call it a "sense of humor," for lack of a better term—that compels them to try to arouse a response from those cows, maybe by doing something like yelling, "Mooooo!"

Well, stop it. You think you're being funny, but you're really just ruining someone's dinner.

Those cows are going to the slaughterhouse. Remember how you felt back in school (we're guessing college) when the teacher told you to stop making farting noises with your armpit? You felt picked on, stressed out—maybe even a little angry. That's something similar to how a cow feels when it's been rounded up with a bunch of other confused cows and taken away from its familiar surroundings in a giant, noisy machine. Livestock such as cows, pigs, and sheep can get stressed, and when stressed-out livestock becomes meat, it tastes bad.

When an animal is stressed—psychologically (say, by mooing motorists or by other disruptions experienced on the way to the slaughterhouse) or physically (say, by fighting, which happens when animals are put in pens with other animals they don't know)—it gets tense, worn out, or exhausted. This causes the glycogen stores, or short-term energy, in its muscles to be used up.

If the animal is slaughtered before the glycogen levels are restored, the meat will have a high pH level, or not enough lactic acid. In the meat-processing industry, this is known as dark, firm, dry (DFD) meat. DFD meat is sticky and has less flavor. It is also more susceptible to microorganisms, which makes its shelf life dangerously short. Another related condition is pale, soft, exudative (PSE) meat. PSE meat, most commonly pork, drips and is soft and mushy. *Mmmmmm!*

Good livestock handlers go to great lengths to ensure that their animals remain as stress-free as possible before slaughter. These measures include hearty meals and plenty of rest for the condemned beasts. After all, nothing is worse for the meat business than bad taste.

Q How many ants make a full meal for a giant anteater?

A How many ants can an anteater eat if an anteater can eat ants? How about a whopping thirty-five thousand per day? And when the giant anteater can't eat ants, it will settle for termites and consume about an equal number.

That sounds like an awful lot of insects, but keep in mind that the average ant or termite weighs only three milligrams. So despite the volume of insects that it eats, the voracious anteater is consuming less than an ounce of food at every meal. Fortunately, the anteater's metabolism is very slow. Anteaters typically maintain a body temperature of only 90.9 degrees Fahrenheit—one of the lowest temps in the animal kingdom—which enables them to thrive on this highly specialized diet.

How do they eat? After locating a large nest of ants or termites, an anteater gouges a hole with its powerful front claws, pokes its nose in, and starts chowing down. Its long, snaky tongue is the ideal utensil for scooping up those tiny ants. Coated with sticky black hairs, the tongue extends more than two feet from the anteater's mouth and flicks in and out at the amazing rate of one hundred and fifty times a minute. Because it lacks teeth, the anteater also uses its tongue to crush the ants against the roof of its mouth before swallowing.

Why do anteaters eat ants, anyway? According to zoologists, anteaters cannot produce the gastric juices that other mammals use to digest food. Ants and termites are highly acidic and decompose easily in the anteater's stomach without additional acids. Incidentally, anteaters in zoos enjoy a more varied diet, with occasional fruits, vegetables, and honey. But their keepers must make sure they receive the right balance of acid, or the anteaters will not survive.

A full-grown giant anteater is a hefty creature, measuring about four feet high from ground to shoulder and five to seven feet long from nose to tail. Adult males weigh up to ninety pounds, females a little less than that. Anteaters are native to South America. Their primary habitat is east of the Andes Mountains in northwest Argentina and parts of Uruguay.

Though they rarely threaten humans, anteaters have often been hunted for sport and are presently considered endangered by the International Union for Conservation of Nature. Anteaters are excellent conservationists. An anteater will never clean out an entire ant nest at a single sitting. It will always leave enough ants to allow the colony to regenerate, thus ensuring a future meal.

These are pretty smart tactics for a creature with a fairly small brain. Maybe some big-brained mammals should follow the anteater's example and make sure to conserve their own natural resources as wisely.

Q Why does Australia have so many poisonous snakes?

A Many people associate the cute and cuddly koala with Australia. And that's exactly the image the nation's tourism industry wants to tout: cute and cuddly. Deadly and dangerous wouldn't sell as many vacation packages, though it would be more accurate.

Australia is a place that would drive the snake-phobic Indiana Jones to the brink of insanity—there are snakes, snakes, and more snakes, many of which are poisonous. Of the approximately six hundred known venomous snakes in the world, a whopping sixty-one reside in Australia, according to the University of Sydney. And the Australia Venom Research Unit reports that eight of the ten most toxic land snakes on the planet are native to the continent.

Cute and cuddly? We think not. Thirty-five percent of the snake species in Australia are poisonous. Why does this continent host so many scary slitherers? Hundreds of millions of years ago, Australia was part of the supercontinent Gondwana, which also included South America, Africa, India, New Zealand, and Antarctica. Gondwana began to break up one hundred and fifty million years ago, and Australia snapped off altogether about fifty million years ago.

The snakes that were on the terrain now known as Australia included those from the Elapidae family, a group that had many venomous varieties. Once this land mass became completely surrounded by water, the snakes had nowhere to go. So they developed ways to survive on this biodiverse continent, which has a rain forest, vast deserts, and the largest coral reef on the planet.

As is the case with natural selection, the strongest varieties lasted; many of today's venomous serpents are descendents of the poisonous Gondwana castaways.

Australia's venomous snakes come in a variety of lengths and colors, and they reside in many of the continent's environments. The deadliest—not just on Australia, but on the entire planet—is the inland taipan. This snake, part of the ancient Elapidae family, has venom potent enough to kill one hundred humans in a single bite. Close behind on the venom chart are the eastern brown snake and mainland tiger snake, which also hail from the dreaded Elapidae clan. Both can seriously ruin a vacation.

But don't let these snakes—or the continent's other poisonous critters, such as the box jellyfish or the funnel web spider—scare you away. If you visit Australia, the main predator you'll need to beware of is the human—specifically, those who are driving cars. Auto accidents cause more deaths each year in Australia than all of its poisonous creatures combined.

Q Why do moths eat clothes?

A Did you find a few holes in that expensive cashmere V-neck? Well, even a moth's gotta eat.

Still, most species of moths prefer to feed on plants rather than clothes. Ever heard of the bollworm? These guys are notorious for causing major damage to ornamental trees and shrubs, as well as commercial crops of cotton, tomatoes, and beans.

The moths from the Tineidae family are the ones that are likely to munch on your sweaters, coats, blankets, and comforters—especially if they're stored, undisturbed, in a dark closet or attic. These nocturnal insects tend to avoid light, which is why they are rarely seen.

What does a Tineid moth look like? In general, clothes moths (as they're more commonly known) are about half an inch to an inch long with a dull, mottled, yellowish-beige coloration. They have long, skinny, fringed wings and spiking antennae.

It's important to note that the adult moths aren't the ones that are turning your Irish fisherman's sweater into Swiss cheese—it's their larvae that are doing the damage. These babies (a.k.a. caterpillars) are natural-born scavengers. According to the Missouri Department of Conservation, their food preferences "are unique, even among insects." They achieve this diet because they are among the few organisms that can digest keratin, which is a fibrous animal protein. They mainly feed on fungi and materials of animal origin, including wool, fur, silk, and felt—even hair and feathers.

In their caterpillar stage, clothes moths are creamy white in color and up to half an inch in length. They can do their damage in any number of ways. The larvae of "webbing" clothes moths spin a network of feeding tunnels to make their way across your favorite silk blouse. The larvae of "casemaking" clothes moths can use Grandpa's old army uniform for food and even shelter. These caterpillars collect fiber fragments to construct the flat oval "homes" where they live and pupate into winged adults.

If you end up with an infestation of clothes moths, they probably won't eat their way through everything you own. They tend to avoid cheaper, synthetic fibers, such as polyester or rayon. (Talk about good taste.) That being said, they might be tempted to attack these items if they're soiled with sweat, grease, or food stains.

The trick is to launder (or preferably dry-clean) all woolens and natural-fiber fabrics before storing them away for long periods of time. This will remove the stains and perspiration odors that are attractive to moths. In other words, it will help ensure that your V-neck doesn't become dinner.

Q Why do geese fly in formation?

A A flock of geese migrating south for the winter is a familiar sight (and sound) in many parts of the United States. When the loud honks of the birds draw your eyes skyward, it's almost impossible to avoid noticing that they're flying in a formation shaped like the letter V. Why do they choose this particular shape? It's all about efficiency.

When geese are in a V formation, they aren't flying in straight lines—each goose is stationed slightly above the goose in front of it. As a goose flies, its wings create a wake of air above and behind each wing tip. Scientists call the phenomenon a "wing-tip vortex." Each goose receives a boost of lift from the upper portion of the vortex that's created by the goose in front of it, which means that it doesn't have to work as hard while flying. And saving energy is important when the flock is migrating thousands of miles. The goose at the point of the V, or the lead goose, doesn't have the benefit of wing-tip vortices to conserve its energy. When a lead goose gets tired, it falls back into the formation and another goose takes its place. In addition to saving energy, geese fly in formation to more easily keep track of each other and communicate during the flight.

Until recently, scientists had only theorized about the reasoning behind formation flying. In 2002, a group of French scientists studied a flock of pelicans that had been trained to fly in a V formation and confirmed the aerodynamic and communication benefits.

Combat aircraft fly in formation for a similar reason: It's easier to keep track of each plane. Combat aircraft pilots worry about defending themselves and attacking enemy forces, but when geese are migrating, simply reaching their destination is their main concern. Most of their enemies are waiting on the ground.

Chapter Five

PEOPLE

Q How do you become a witch?

A Let's get something straight: You can't become a witch by being mean, wearing black, or jumping off a roof with a broomstick between your legs. It just doesn't work that way. And if you're considering becoming a witch because you want to learn how to cast a vengeful spell or get up close and personal with Satan, then you're barking up the wrong tree...and you're probably barking mad to boot. Please seek professional help immediately. Thanks.

Now that we've gotten that out of the way, there are a few things you should know about witchcraft, or Wicca, before you make the decision to devote yourself to this misunderstood experience. First, you need to put aside your preconceptions about being a witch (refer to first paragraph). Next, it is important to understand that being a witch means many different things; it involves creativity, empowerment, free thought, peacefulness, spirituality, and being earth-based.

Consider this: The word "witch" is a combination of two Old English terms: *wicce* ("wise one") and *Wicca* ("healer"). In ancient times, witches were admired and respected for their wisdom and ability to heal with herbs. It wasn't until the early thirteen hundreds that witchcraft was declared heresy by—guess who?—the Catholic Church. This resulted in a widespread fear of witches and led to the witch hunts that took place between the late fifteenth and eighteenth centuries.

Once you've freed your mind of old myths, you might want to pick up a book or two—such as *Wicca for Beginners* by Thea Sabin—to learn more about modern or eclectic Wicca, the fastest-growing type of Wicca. It's preferred for its level of freedom from doctrines and the absence of traditional initiation practices. Many Wiccans are vegans, vegetarians, and/or environmentalists, but you don't have to change your diet or lifestyle to become a witch. Wicca is about the mind, body, and spirit, along with a code of ethics and a few principles that some witches share. It's not about proselytizing, overuse of magic, exclusion, or controlling others, nor is it dualistic, satanic, or Goth. Respect the earth, live in harmony with the seasons, find your own purpose, and create your own path. *Poof!* You're a witch.

While the majority of today's Wiccan churches gladly welcome those who are interested in both traditional and eclectic Wiccan, most church "administration offices" have a process in place to help separate the serious inquiries from the crackpot questions. If you're serious about wanting to become a witch, here's some contact information for two well-known Wiccan churches:

New Wiccan Church International
PO Box 162046
Sacramento, CA 95816
NWCoutreach@yahoo.com
www.newwiccanchurch.net

Church and School of Wicca
PO Box 297-IN
Hinton, WV 25951
School@citynet.net
www.wicca.org

Q Who invented cigarettes?

A A bunch of seventeenth-century beggars, bless their enterprising souls.

In 1614, King Philip III of Spain established Seville as the tobacco capital of the world when he mandated that all tobacco grown in the Spanish New World be shipped there to control its flow and prevent a glut. Seville specialized in cigars, but beggars found they could cobble together cigar scraps, wrap them in paper, and make passable cigarettes, called *papeletes* ("little papers").

You can trace the growth of the cigarette in Britain and America to the cultural ramifications of wars that wracked Europe between the French Revolution in the late eighteenth century and the Crimean War in the mid-nineteenth century. During the French Revolution, the French masses made a social statement by smoking *cigaritos*. Produced from the tobacco that was scared up from leftover snuff, cigars, and pipes, these *cigaritos* were unlike the aristocracy's snuff. In the mid-eighteen hundreds, the cigarette was brought to Britain by soldiers who had returned from the Crimean War, where they had learned of cigarettes from their French and Turkish allies.

Cigarettes began to rise in popularity in the United States during the Civil War. Soldiers received tobacco in their rations and enjoyed rolling their own smokes with the sweet tobacco that was grown in the Southeast. (The first cigarette tax was imposed during the Civil War.) By the late eighteen hundreds, cigarettes were being hand-rolled in factories in England, Russia, Germany, and the United States.

In 1880, the industry was revolutionized by the invention of the cigarette-rolling machine. This device not only could produce many times the number of cigarettes as a human could roll by hand, but it also could do so more cheaply. James Bonsack, a Virginian, invented the machine, which created a long tube of paper-wrapped tobacco that was cut into cigarette lengths.

A few years after the machine was invented, tobacco industrialist James Duke licensed it and worked out the bugs. Less than a decade later, Duke was manufacturing four million cigarettes a day. Accompanying increased production was the introduction of a more easily and deeply inhaled variety of tobacco, as well as plenty of advertising.

About forty years after Bonsack's invention, cigarette production had increased roughly thirtyfold, leaving the previously popular cigars in the dust. And at the turn of this century, an estimated 5.5 trillion smokes were manufactured annually worldwide. Hey, got a light?

Q Who got the first tattoo?

A The story of the first tattoo does not involve a bachelor party. Incredible, we know.

The first tattoo was probably an accident. Not the kind of accident that leads to the name Roxie above the biceps—a real accident. Tattoos have been around for several thousand years and might have started when someone rubbed a wound with dirt, soot, or ash and noticed that the mark stayed after the injury had healed.

For the sake of giving this question a definitive answer, we turn to Iceman, who sports the oldest tats ever seen on a body. (And with a name like that, he'd fit right in on MTV!) In 1991, the frozen and amazingly well-preserved remains of a Bronze Age man were found between Austria and Italy in the Tyrolean Alps. Iceman, as he was dubbed, is believed to be more than five thousand years old, and he clearly has a series of lines tattooed on his lower back, ankles, knees, and foot. It is thought that the tattoos were applied for medicinal purposes, to reduce pain.

Over time, tattoos evolved into symbols or designs that have meaning. Mummified Egyptian women dating back to 2100 BC have patterns of lines and dots on their bodies that were applied, historians believe, to enhance fertility and provide protection. All tattoos in this period were thought of as a way of connecting the body to a higher power.

When did someone finally step it up and go with something more intricate than lines and dots? That question is impossible to answer conclusively, but a Nubian mummy, circa 400 BC, has a tattoo of Bes, the Egyptian god of fertility and revelry, on her thigh. Several Egyptian paintings from this period depict dancers and musicians with Bes tattoos on their thighs.

Tattoos have gone in and out of style. In early Rome, for instance, they were decidedly out of style and were even banned among the general populace because they were thought to taint the body's purity. Back then, body ink was reserved for criminals (as a form of punishment, like a scarlet letter) and slaves (so that they could be identified if they escaped). Eventually, attitudes changed—Roman soldiers began getting tattoos after fighting a rugged army of Britons who wore their body art like badges of honor.

Today, it's hard to find a professional basketball player or a musical performer who isn't sporting ink. There are even reality shows about the studios—don't say "parlors," because it isn't cool and you'll sound like a crusty old sailor—where tattoos are applied. A Harris Interactive poll in 2008 revealed that about half of Americans between ages eighteen and twenty-nine have a tattoo. No word on how much of that ink was still fresh the morning after a bachelor—or bachelorette—party.

Q What's up with eunuchs?

A Not much. If the notion of having an up-close fling with a blade is enough to make you cross your legs in panic, imagine enduring life as a castrated man. Surprisingly, though, the excruciatingly painful and gruesome rite of castration sometimes led to unusual social significance in early cultures.

In Chinese dynasties of the eighth century BC, eunuchs were viewed as loyal court servants; the possibility of these servants seeking personal gain through romantic trysts or producing children was eliminated with the swing of a blade. Often, eunuchs were pooled from batches of slaves, prisoners of war, and children who were sold by their families. Considering these humble roots, being a eunuch wasn't a bad gig. As a liaison between the court and public, he could parlay his position into one of stature within the government.

In the Ottoman Empire of the sixteenth and seventeenth centuries, eunuchs served as harem-keepers, managing the needs of kept women who provided sexual services to the ruling official or sultan. Since eunuchs weren't regarded as true men, they could be trusted by the sultan to be around harem women. They protected the harem, delivered criminal sentences to women, promoted females to higher ranks, and purchased ladies-in-waiting.

Italian eunuchs in the seventeenth and eighteenth centuries underwent their transformations for a different reason: to retain high falsetto voices for singing. Since females were prohibited from performing, about four thousand adolescent boys, or castrati, assumed the alto parts, and some were considered among the greatest singers in Italian opera.

Nowadays, eunuchs lack the prestige they once enjoyed in Italy. India's *hijras* are regarded as horrifying creatures. They seek refuge among their own poor, cloistered community, which functions at the lowest levels of Indian society. *Hijras* are often frustrated homosexuals who are unable to fit in with the populace and, thus, resort to prostitution or begging. Their begging routine consists of wandering the streets wearing gaudy clothing and makeup, singing, and threatening to expose themselves if they're not given money.

Eunuchs in India and elsewhere in the world might be shunned by today's mainstream society, but at least they have each other. There's even a Web site (www.eunuch.org) that serves as a source of support for the eunuch community. These eunuchs might even tell you that less is more.

Q Have zoos ever had human beings on exhibit?

A The London Zoo made a startling announcement on August 17, 2005: a "flock of *Homo sapiens*" would be on exhibit for four days that month, "cared for by our experienced keepers and ... entertained through various forms of enrichment."

Of course, the zoo's temporary human exhibit, which featured a volunteer group of five women and three men, was conducted with tongue firmly planted in anthropological cheek. But ninety-nine years earlier, a human exhibit at the Bronx Zoo triggered an uproar. On September 8, 1906, a sign appeared outside the zoo's monkey house: THE AFRICAN PYGMY, OTA BENGA. AGE 23 YEARS. HEIGHT 4'11''. WEIGHT 103 POUNDS.

Inside, visitors saw a slight young man dressed in white trousers and a khaki coat peering at them from behind the bars. His feet were bare, and his smile revealed teeth filed to points in the manner of his people, the Batwa tribe of the Belgian Congo. Sometimes, he played with an orangutan named Dohong. Other times, he shot arrows at straw targets. Occasionally, he was allowed out of the cage to buy soda from the snack bar with money he had earned by posing for photographers.

Over the next few days, thousands gathered at the monkey cage to watch Ota Benga. The crowds became nearly unmanageable, and clergymen registered their objections with the New York Times. "The person responsible for this exhibition degrades himself as much as he degrades the African," thundered the Reverend R. S. MacArthur of Harlem's Calvary Baptist Church.

What did Ota Benga think of all this? He probably knew more about white people, or muzungu as he called them, than they knew about him. After all, he had been on display once before—at the 1904 St. Louis World's Fair, where he and several fellow pygmies recreated their native village as part of the fair's Living Exhibits program. But there, he had been among other human beings; at the Bronx Zoo, his presence in the monkey cage implied something quite different.

William Hornaday, the head of the zoo, defended the exhibit. He said Ota Benga was fed and treated well. Still, as one anonymous visitor put it, "There's something here I don't like."

Ota eventually was removed and taken by a sympathetic minister to live at the Howard Colored Orphan Asylum in Lynchburg, Virginia. After several years, he learned English and acquired a job in a tobacco factory. Despite his attempts to fit in, Ota Benga never quite adjusted to the ways of the muzungu. In March 1916, he went into a forest, performed a ceremonial dance around a fire, and shot himself in the heart with a borrowed gun.

Q Who is John Doe?

A There is no single John Doe from whom the rest have followed. The name is today what it has always been: a placeholder. John Doe is used when a person's name is unknown or when a person wishes to remain anonymous.

The name first appeared in legal proceedings known as actions of ejectment, which were common in England from the early thirteen hundreds until 1852 and also were used in the United States. In these proceedings, John Doe was a fictional name for the plaintiff; the name substituted for the defendant was the equally fictional Richard Roe.

An action of ejectment could be brought to the court by a person who had been thrown out of his own property by a trespasser or who had rented his property to a tenant who stopped paying rent and refused to leave. Either way, the person occupying the property had no right to be there, and the owner wanted him out.

Enter John Doe and Richard Roe. The property owner claimed in court to have granted a lease to John Doe; John Doe, in turn, claimed to have been kept from using the property by Richard Roe. A letter was then sent to Richard Roe, urging him to appear in court. Because there wasn't a Richard Roe—at least not at that address—the real-life defendant came to the court to speak on his own behalf. The court allowed this, at which point the fictional lease became moot and the subject turned to the ownership of the land's title.

Is your head spinning yet? The process was overly complex, and it's anyone's guess why a person couldn't use his own name to argue property issues. England's Common Law Procedure Act, which was passed in 1852, did away with the action of ejectment and streamlined eviction proceedings. American law, however, continued the practice well into the twentieth century, using the same proxies for actual citizens.

Who came up with these names? It is likely that John and Richard were chosen because they were common English names. The origins of Doe and Roe are murkier. They might refer to deer: A doe is a female deer, and a roe is a type of deer native to Europe. Or they might have been chosen because one indicates deer and the other fish ("roe" can also refer to a mass of fish eggs), the thought process being that both deer and fish were commonly poached. Either way, the origins seem to be as anonymous as the names themselves.

Q How famous do you have to be to go by one name?

A As it turns out, you don't have to be famous at all to go by one name. In fact, the only requirement appears to be a massively inflated sense of your own importance. If you are considering pursuing fame and fortune via the one-word pseudonym, perhaps you can learn from the self-absorbed trailblazers who came before you.

The first thing to know about one-name celebrities is that the over-whelming majority of them are in the music industry. They fall into two categories: those who make up bizarre stage names for themselves (such as Slash, Flea, and Eminem) and those whose real first names are bizarre enough (such as Seal, Madonna, and Jewel).

Regardless of the group to which your celebrity role models belong, they all seem to have one thing in common: They had their pretentious nicknames before they were famous. Gordon Sumner, for example, was calling himself Sting before he joined the rock band The Police. Prince Rogers Nelson's first album, *For You,* bears only his first name, back when most people could care less about him one way or another. And then you have U2—a band that was nutty enough to have not one, but two single-name members before it recorded an album: Bono and The Edge.

Naturally, there is a certain amount of risk involved in deciding to adopt one name. The last thing you want is to be working as a garbage man and explaining to the customers along your route that they should now refer to you as Shimmer or Justice. Here's a quick tip: If you can't sing or play a musical instrument, it's probably best to stick with the name that your parents gave you.

Q Whatever happened to Neanderthals?

A Once upon a time, about one hundred thousand years ago, there were people who lived in the mountains of Europe. Their bodies were short and stocky, and they had barrel chests, bowed legs, and sloping shoulders. Their faces were characterized by thick protruding foreheads, big noses, and receding chins. They used tools made of bone, stone, and wood; wore clothing consisting of animal hide; and cooked with fire. When one of them died, the body was interred in a ceremony and sometimes strewn with flowers. They may have even played music with flutes that were fashioned from hollow bones.

Then, about forty thousand years ago, some very interesting neighbors showed up. They were smaller and slimmer, and sported longer legs and narrower fingers. They also had a more pronounced jaw, which made it easier for them to articulate a variety of sounds. Among their innovations were language, jewelry, art, and tools with sharp, finely honed blades. After another ten thousand years, the first inhabitants had disappeared. But the later arrivals flourished. If you want to see one of their descendants, just look in the mirror. That's you—*Homo sapiens.*

And what happened to *Homo neanderthalensis?* Neanderthals and *Homo sapiens* share a common ancestor, *Homo erectus,* who evolved in Africa about two million years ago. For decades, paleontologists wondered if the two groups had been biologically close enough to interbreed. In other words, scientists theorized that Neanderthals didn't actually die out—they suspected that they're still with us, in our genes. In 2006, however, biologists at the Max Planck Institute for Evolutionary Anthropology in Leipzig, Germany, and the Joint Genome Institute in Walnut Creek, California, retrieved DNA from a fragment of a thirty-eight-thousand-year-old Neanderthal femur bone and concluded that it was highly unlikely that Neanderthals and *Homo sapiens* produced mutual offspring. Though related, they were probably two distinct species, which would have made interbreeding impossible.

So what did happen? One dark scenario casts *Homo sapiens* as war-like aggressors who attacked and killed the peaceable Neanderthals. Dramatic as this theory is, researchers consider it as unlikely as Neanderthal-*sapiens* love children. Another possible culprit is one that we're worrying about today: climate change. The disappearance of the Neanderthals coincided with the end of the last ice age. Receding glaciers altered the landscape and affected animal migration patterns. Perhaps Neanderthals found survival difficult in this warmer world. Disease, too, may have played a role in their extinction.

In the end, no one really knows why Neanderthals died out. But our interest in their demise has led us to uncover a wealth of information about their lives. Like us, Neanderthals had big brains. They lived in social groups and performed rituals, just as we do today.

Contemporary humans are the only species of *Homo* left on the planet, and while we may glory in our singularity, being one of a kind can be a little lonely. This may be why our imaginations are drawn so powerfully to the ancient campsites of these distant relations, who were lost forever just as our own history began.

Q Who created time zones?

A On a pleasant July evening in 1876, Sir Sanford Fleming was waiting in a railroad station in Bandoran, Ireland, for a train that had been listed in his *Railway Travelers Guide* as due at 5:35. When the train failed to arrive, he inquired at the ticket office and learned that it stopped there at 5:35 in the morning, not 5:35 in the evening. Fleming might have just fired off an irritated letter to the editor of the *Guide;* instead, he decided it was time to change time.

Up to that point in history, the sun had ruled time. Earth rotates at approximately 17.36 miles per minute, which means that if you move thirty-five miles west of your present location, noon will arrive about two minutes earlier. Going the same distance east, it would come two minutes later. Confusing? Yes. But back in horse-and-buggy days, keeping precise track of time wasn't really an issue. What difference did a few minutes make when your only goal was to arrive at your destination before sundown?

The invention of the railroad altered this ancient perception of time forever. To run efficiently, railroads needed a schedule, and a schedule needed a timetable, and every minute did indeed count. Fleming, who had worked as a railroad surveyor in Canada, was even more aware of the confusion over time than most people. Each railroad company used its own time, which was set according to noon at company headquarters. A weary traveler might be faced with five or six clocks at the station. Which one was correct?

Fleming came up with what he believed to be an ingenious solution. Earth would be divided into twenty-four sectors, like the sections of an orange, each fifteen degrees latitude apart. Each section would become a time zone, its clocks set exactly one hour earlier than the preceding zone.

Though Fleming's proposal was a model of common sense, he had a hard time convincing people to buy into it. The United States was an early adaptor, mandating four continental time zones in

1883. A year later, President Chester Arthur assembled the International Prime Meridian Conference in Washington, D.C. Twenty-five nations were invited and nineteen showed. They chose the Royal Observatory at Greenwich, England, as the prime meridian because it was already used by the British Navy to set time.

It wasn't until 1929, however, that standard time zones were instituted throughout the world. Fleming also proposed the use of a twenty-four-hour clock, which would have meant that his evening train would have been scheduled to arrive at 17:35 rather than 5:35. This never caught on, except in the military and hospitals.

The sun remains our touchstone when it comes to time. We still recognize the twin poles of noon and midnight—one light, the other dark. Each, however, has the same number affixed to its name, which reminds us that on this planet, what goes around will always come around again.

Chapter Six

BODY SCIENCE

Q Why do people yawn?

A Chances are good that at some point as you peruse this book, you'll break out into a yawn. It's not because you're anything less than riveted, although it might help if you're a little bored. A yawn is simply one of nature's irresistible urges. Why? Ask a doctor who has spent years studying the structure and function of the human body, and after much theorizing, you'll probably get a dressed-up version of "I dunno."

There are many theories for why we yawn—and why we pandiculate, which is when we stretch and yawn at the same time—but they have holes as gaping as the mouth of an unrepentant yawner.

One theory is that we yawn to expel a buildup of carbon dioxide from our lungs—that the yawn is a maneuver that lets the body take in a larger-than-usual amount of oxygen and displace excess carbon dioxide. But if this were the only reason for a yawn, people who already have enough oxygen would never do it. Studies have demonstrated that increasing the amount of oxygen or decreasing the amount of carbon dioxide in a room does not decrease the frequency of yawns.

Even if it's not entirely satisfying, the oxygen/carbon dioxide theory can be tied to another popular explanation for the phenomenon: boredom and fatigue. When we're tired or bored, we begin to take breaths that are shallower, so it would make sense that we'd need the occasional influx of extra oxygen. But why, then, are yawns contagious? Fifty-five percent of people yawn when they see someone else do it; for many, even thinking or reading about yawning will cause it.

Yet another theory contends that the yawn is a vestigial habit that has been passed down to us from our distant ancestors—a relic that shows how humans communicated before developing language. Perhaps we yawned to intimidate by showing our teeth or as another kind of signal to our fellow humans. Yawning could have been a means of synchronizing a group as it passed from person to person. A similar explanation suggests that yawning actually increases alertness, which could help explain why yawning is contagious—the more alert a group, the more effective it would be at fighting or hunting.

There are also theories that yawning helps cool the brain, keeps the lungs from collapsing, and helps equalize ear pressure. Whatever the reason we yawn, it is certainly ingrained in us from an early age: Fetuses begin yawning at eleven weeks. And unless an eleven-week-old fetus is thoughtful enough to be bored, there's got to be something more to yawning than that.

Q Is there a "baby genius" sperm bank?

A There was, in San Diego. People called it the Nobel Prize Sperm Bank (its official name was the Repository for Germinal Choice). Not every customer visited because hubby was firing blanks: Some women—and couples—simply wanted to increase the chances that their children would be exceptional.

Some history: Up through the 1970s, women who couldn't get pregnant visited doctors who injected them with sperm via a syringe. Whose sperm? Sometimes it was the doctor's, sometimes a medical student's. Records were not kept. It wasn't exactly an ideal situation for prospective parents. So when millionaire Robert K. Graham advertised his Nobel Prize Sperm Bank and said that he had convinced three to five laureates to donate, newspapers, magazines, and customers came calling.

Graham, who said he was dedicated to improving the species, created a catalogue, coding his sperm donors—no real names were ever revealed—and listing their accomplishments. Besides Nobel Prize winners, Graham said those who gave sperm included brilliant scientists, athletes, and overachievers in many other fields. Between 1982 and 1997, when Graham died, 215 babies were born through his intercession. The Repository for Germinal Choice closed in 1999.

While the "baby genius" approach was often mocked, Graham's unique sperm bank had an unexpected side effect: Doctors and entrepreneurs were made aware that women wanted to know about their sperm donors. Height, intelligence, general health, musical ability, and other characteristics may or may not be inherited, but female clients of sperm banks found comfort in the knowledge that their child's biological father was not a criminal, ugly, or a carrier of disease, among other negative traits.

Because of the fear of AIDS in the 1980s, it became common practice for sperm banks to record certain facts about their anonymous sperm donors and to allow patrons to choose whose sperm they would accept.

Q How many diapers does a baby go through before being potty-trained?

A The average newborn runs through (no pun intended) about twelve to sixteen diapers per day, according to Diapering Decisions, a supplier of cloth diapers. If we define a newborn as being two weeks old or younger, a baby goes through 168 to 224 diapers in just the first fourteen days of life.

Luckily, the pace slows a bit after that. Between three and six months of age, you'll change a baby ten to twelve times a day; between six and nine months, ten times a day; from nine months to the end of the first year, eight times a day; and up to eighteen months, count on six to eight changes a day.

When will it end?

That depends on your kid. It might be as early as two years; it might take as long as four. WebMD.com says that the average for boys is thirty-eight months; for girls, who seem to do about everything earlier than boys do, the average is thirty-six months.

Thus, you'll change little Georgie between 8,008 and 10,150 times before he's ready to tackle the potty. Little Susan will soil about four hundred fewer diapers; you'll change her between 7,672 and 9,702 times.

If you start the potty-training process early and remain diligent, Georgie and Susan will beat those averages. Good thing, too. With disposable diapers averaging twenty cents apiece, your baby's bottom can drain you of $1.40 per day. If the little bugger does his or her business on the toilet, it's good business for you.

Q If you lose your sense of smell, do you still have food cravings?

A When a stuffy head cold dulls your enjoyment of a slice of your favorite pizza, you are experiencing what life is like for those afflicted with anosmia, or loss of smell. It can be brought on temporarily (by that head cold or allergies) or more permanently (by a virus, medication, nasal disorders, or a head injury). About sixteen million Americans deal with chronic smell or taste dysfunction. And yes, it does diminish food cravings—but that's only part of what it can do to you.

Although smell loss is not addressed by researchers with the same urgency as sight or hearing loss, it probably should be. The sense of smell contributes greatly to one's ability to lead a full and healthy life. On a physical level, smell helps us sense danger (such as smoke in a fire outbreak) and keep us out of harm's way (it can stop us from chowing down on spoiled food or toxic substances). On a psychological level, chronic anosmia can have a negative effect on moods, behaviors, memories, and even sexual health.

But the topic here is food cravings. While a lack of cravings might seem like an advantage in our weight-conscious world, those who have lost their sniffing ability have been known, at least initially, to gain weight—up to 10 percent of their body weight, in fact. Why? Let's consider smell's role in eating.

When an odor enters the nose, it's greeted by millions of receptor cells in an area at the back of the nasal cavity called the olfactory epithelium. These receptor cells connect to receptor cells in the olfactory bulb, which sends electrical signals to areas of the brain—including the appetite center in the hypothalamus—which is connected to the satiety center. The satiety center interprets the signal and informs the brain when you are full. This response is direct and quicker than the satiety signals that the stomach sends to the brain. For those lacking the sense of smell, there is a breakdown in the olfactory satiety feedback mechanism. In short, anosmia sufferers have difficulty gauging when to stop eating.

Furthermore, those with anosmia typically are unable to distinguish flavors, which is another factor that can lead to weight gain.

Chewing food releases odor molecules that stimulate the olfactory mechanism, enhancing the eating experience. People who have anosmia sometimes overcompensate for the lack of smell—they try to kick-start any kind of sensitivity by eating more.

So the next time you catch a whiff of freshly made donuts, don't try to stave off your craving by plugging your proboscis. Remember, the ability to experience life's bouquet of fragrances—even those of a fattening donut—helps keep you healthy.

Q Why do dead bodies float?

A You're in your first year at Gangsters College. After doing a boffo job on your presentation on brass knuckles in your Tools of the Trade 101 class, you've settled in for a riveting lecture on cement boots. And you're shocked—this isn't going to be the breeze you expected. Professor Fat Anthony teaches you that if you don't weigh down a body properly before you throw it into a waterway, it can float to the top. Wait a second—that didn't happen to the guys from *The Sopranos* when they threw Big Pussy overboard!

It's crazy, but true: Bodies that are laden with weight that is equivalent to or greater than the body's shouldn't float to the top. However, bodies that aren't weighted may float for a while. Why? For the most part, it comes down to gas—and not the type that gangsters would use to torch a rat's house. We're talking about gases that form from bacteria in the body during decomposition, including methane, hydrogen sulfide, and carbon dioxide.

Bacteria in our bodies love to eat. When we're alive, they eat the food in our systems; when we die and there is no food left in our systems, they eat us. Bacteria break down what they eat and produce gas. This gas has no way of being expelled from a corpse, so it causes the body to bloat and, thus, float (if it happens to be in water). Once you have a floater, it's going to remain on the water's surface until there is enough decomposition of the flesh to allow the gas to escape.

Not all parts of the body inflate at the same rate. The torso, which is home to the most bacteria, becomes more bloated than the arms, legs, and head. This is partly why a body always floats face-down. The arms, legs, and head can only fall forward from a dead body, so the corpse tends to flip, with the less-gas-filled limbs dangling beneath the giant gas ball of the chest and abdomen.

Depending on the situation, the speed of the decomposition process can vary. For instance, cold water slows down decomposition considerably, while warm water speeds up the bacteria feast. It's a gory sight. Not even the fishes want to sleep with such a thing.

Q Why does spicy food make us sweat?

A Five-alarm chili! Your tongue burns, the veins on your neck stand out, and sweat pours down your face with every bite. Still, you can't stop eating.

Why does super-spicy food hurt so bad and taste so good? The culprit is a chemical substance called capsaicin, which is found largely in the white membrane enclosing a pepper's seeds. Capsaicin, a.k.a. *trans*-8-methyl-*N*-vanillyl-6-nonenamide, has been the subject of some pretty intense scientific research. Basically, capsaicin irritates the nerve receptors in the tongue and mucous membranes of the mouth. The brain interprets this tingling sensation as burning and says, "Wow, we're getting hot! Better set off the sprinkler system to cool down." Hence, the sweat.

In other words, capsaicin doesn't literally burn; it just feels like it does. Of course, that's not much comfort if you get it in your eyes. Always wash your hands after handling hot peppers; should you forget and accidentally touch your eyes, flush them with water immediately. A compress soaked in milk or yogurt is soothing, too. Dairy products contain casein, a protein that defuses the irritation caused by chili peppers, this is probably why yogurt has been an accompaniment to hot Indian curries.

Capsaicin itself has no color, odor, or flavor. It's the way it is combined with other ingredients that gives it its unmistakable zing. And capsaicin can be as effective in healing pain as it is in causing it: Capsaicin has a slightly numbing effect on non-mucous membranes. Many pharmaceutical companies now add it to topical creams that are used to alleviate pain due to osteoarthritis, psoriasis, diabetes, and other chronic disorders.

And if you still prefer to eat your hot peppers rather than wear them, you'll be glad to know they're an excellent source of vitamins C and A, beta-carotene, potassium, iron, and dietary fiber. They've even been known to kill bacteria that are associated with ulcers. So dig in! Whether you get your kicks from tostadas with salsa, Schezwan noodles, or chicken vindaloo, don't sweat chili peppers. They're good for you.

Q Did teachers really tie students' hands behind their backs to discourage them from being left-handed?

A In July 2007, scientists announced they had discovered the gene that probably causes people to be left-handed. This might not seem like a big deal—unless you're among the 5 to 10 percent of the world's adult population that's left-handed.

Being left-handed has long held a social stigma. The French *gauche* ("left") is used in English to describe a person who is graceless or crude. In Gaelic, left-handed people are *ciotógs* ("awkward"). Conversely, in most languages, "right" means correct, just, or proper. In some cultures, it is acceptable to eat only with the right hand; the left hand is solely for cleaning yourself. Scissors, knives, and a host of other utensils and tools are designed for the right-handed. Some researchers believe that lefthanders may die younger than righties, that they have an increased risk of developing breast cancer, and that they are at higher risk for various neurological or mental disorders.

Given this taint, parents and teachers have long discouraged children from writing with their left hands. But preventing a child from using a preferred hand is difficult. If verbal admonishment or moving the pencil to the right hand didn't work, some parents and teachers took harsher measures. Some adults harbor childhood memories of having their left hands smacked with rulers. And some teachers really did tie left-handed students' hands behind them or to their desks to force use of the right hand.

Comments in an informal survey by the Left-Handers Club in the United Kingdom and on *Gauche!,* a Web site for lefthanders that is run by the University of Indiana, include stories from students who were punished or ridiculed for trying to use their left hands to write, sew, operate machinery, or play musical instruments. Not only did this result in traumatic memories, but it often didn't work. Lefthanders who survived unscathed sometimes still have trouble writing neatly.

Today, the general consensus is that it's best to let a child use the hand he or she prefers. Still, it may be difficult for a lefthanded child to learn various tasks, such as writing, from a righthander. Luckily, there are numerous resources and tools to assist teachers and parents.

And lefties can take comfort in knowing that they're part of a long list of luminaries, one that includes presidents Ronald Reagan, John F. Kennedy, Gerald Ford, and Bill Clinton, artist Michelangelo, scientist Albert Einstein, astronaut Buzz Aldrin, and musician Paul McCartney.

Q Why do we get baby teeth, then adult teeth, then wisdom teeth?

A While a fetus is still floating around inside its mother, its teeth have begun the process of calcification. Baby teeth (also called deciduous teeth because they eventually fall out) start breaking through a child's gums six months to one year after birth. They are replaced by secondary teeth, but the fact that they will fall out doesn't mean that deciduous teeth should be treated as throwaway chompers. Proper care of deciduous teeth helps ensure that the secondary teeth will come in healthy and strong.

At around age six, deciduous teeth start living up to their name. Baby teeth are smaller in size and fewer in number than adult teeth so that they can fit into a child's small mouth. Once a child's head has grown, his or her jawline has expanded enough to accommodate the larger secondary set. Baby teeth loosen one by one and break free from the gums. Adult teeth (also called *succedaneous* teeth, Latin for "substituted" or "to follow after") can remain functional for a lifetime—right down to your very last T-bone steak—assuming they receive proper care.

So what are the extra molars that appear after just about every other body part has finished growing? They are wisdom teeth, named as such because they pop up once a person reaches the age of maturity and wisdom—though they should not be held up as proof of either quality. Wisdom teeth start forming during childhood and usually erupt between ages seventeen and twenty-five. Some people never grow them at all. Whether a person gets these extra molars is a question of genetics; about 35 percent of the population stays wisdom teeth–free.

Wisdom teeth typically vary in number from one to four. In rare cases, the number can be even higher, which is a mystery that scientists have yet to unravel. Wisdom teeth are often removed because they can be extremely painful and can cause serious oral problems. A small percentage of the population—around 15 percent, according to the American Association of Oral and Maxillofacial Surgeons—will grow properly functioning wisdom teeth; for these lucky few, extraction is not necessary.

Many scientists believe that wisdom teeth are needless holdovers from a time when humans hung out in or underneath trees, eating leaves, berries, nuts, roots, and tough meat. Our teeth suffered a lot more wear and tear in those days, so a third set of molars would have been useful.

Now, the only remaining mystery is: What does the Tooth Fairy do with all of the chompers she gathers? Stay tuned.

Q Why do people get carsick?

A If you're reading this in a car, the answer will get weirdly metaphysical. In fact, if you're reading this in a car, there's a fair chance that you're feeling quite ill right now. This is called motion sickness. Car sickness is just the term for motion sickness that occurs when you happen to be in a car. When you're on a plane, the same symptoms can be called air sickness. Sailors can get sea sick, and astronauts are afflicted with space sickness. And if you're playing a video game, it's called simulator sickness.

Here's what's happening. We don't just detect motion with our eyes; our peepers notice things that are moving around us, sure, but we also use our inner ears. When our head moves, the gear in our inner ear (or "bony labyrinth," which is a much more enjoyable phrase) tells the brain what's happening.

Say you're reading this in a car and feeling ill. It is believed that this is happening because your brain is receiving conflicting messages from its motion detectors. Your eyes are focused on this page and the words aren't moving, so the eyes are telling the brain, "We're not moving." But the motion detectors in the bony labyrinth are telling the brain, "We are moving because our head is bouncing around."

Let's face it—the brain has a lot of work to do and is understandably vexed by these two conflicting reports. But why do you feel sick? One theory is that the brain thinks the body has been poisoned and that either the eyes or ears are hallucinating, so it starts up the vomit routine in order to get rid of any ingested toxins.

Some possible remedies? Close your eyes to eliminate the conflict. Sit in the front seat of the car and focus on the horizon—this ensures that your eyes see the motion that your body feels. Take some anti-nausea medicine. And for goodness sake, put down this book and read it at home!

Q Why do we have eyebrows?

A Quick. Draw a face. That's right—two eyes, a nose, and a mouth. You can turn the mouth up for a smile or down for a frown. But somehow your little face seems to lack expression. What's missing?

Add two short lines above the eyes. That's it! You can arch them up to convey surprise, even them out to indicate boredom, or pull them down into V to show anger. With eyebrows, your face seems more alive—more, well, human.

Is that why we have eyebrows? To serve as a visual communication system? Actually, yes. According to anthropologists, one reason our highly mobile brows evolved was to give us the ability to signal each other when words just wouldn't do. When a predator was lurking nearby, for instance, or when teaching children who were too young for verbal communication. Cave mama's angry V said, "Keep away from the fire, kid!"

The other function of eyebrows is pretty obvious. Take a look at our ancestor Cro-Magnon man: His big, bushy protruding unibrow protected his eyes from falling leaves, volcanic ash, prehistoric flying insects, and other threats to his vision. Brows also collected sweat when he was out hunting mastodons. Brows still function as a runoff system for our sweat. The hairs point outward, to the sides of our face, to guide the droplets away from our eyes. If you have very thin brows or sweat a lot, you know how painful that burning sweat-in-the-eyes sensation can be. That's why dorky headbands evolved as an artificial unibrow.

Do other animals have eyebrows? Many mammals, including dogs and cats, have slight projections on the ridges above the eye sockets. Only primates—especially apes, which are considered to be our nearest evolutionary "cousins"—have recognizable brows. And yes, they use brows to communicate the same way we do. Primate ethologists—those who study the social lives of primates—know that an ape's raised brows can indicate anticipation: "Is that a banana you're holding?" The V can mean, "Better not try taking it away from me." And a quizzical furrow says, "Just kidding, right?"

Why do women have smaller brows than men? One theory is that women needed more expressive faces because they were doing most of the child rearing. Dainty brows have always been considered feminine. Back in the ultra-ladylike 1950s, some fashion mavens almost plucked themselves clean.

Interestingly enough, as men have become more equally involved in raising children, the smoother look has become more popular for them, too. Compare the current crop of clean-browed male movie stars to yesteryear's beetle-browed cowboys and you'll see what we mean.

Will eyebrows ever disappear entirely? Don't count on it. We'll always work up a sweat somehow, and we'll always need to communicate without using words. After all, what's an e-mail without an eyebrowed, winking emoticon that tells us, "Just kidding, right?"

Q Why do we sneeze?

A "Ahhh-chooo!"

"Gesundheit! You just had a sternutation."

"A what?"

"Sternutation. That's the medical term for sneeze."

How did you manage to do that? Chances are, a small particle found its way into your nose. It might have been a bit of pollen, dust, bacteria, a virus, a mite, smoke, or another irritant. Once the nerve cells in the mucous membranes of your nose got wind of it, they released chemicals called histamines. These chemicals acted as messengers, speeding straight to the sneeze center in your brain. (Yes, you really do have a special "sneeze center," located in the area of the brain that connects to the spinal cord, known as the medulla oblongata.) The histamines alerted your brain to the presence of the nasal invaders, and the brain set your body's defense system in motion.

First, your vocal cords closed, causing pressure to build up in your chest and lungs. The pressure built and built and built, and just when you couldn't hold it in any longer, your diaphragm contracted, your eyes shut, your vocal cords snapped open, and air came whooshing out of your mouth and nose at nearly one hundred miles per hour, hopefully carrying the offending particles with it.

Incidentally, sometimes a sneeze begins not in the nose, but in the eyes. If you tend to sneeze whenever you're exposed to bright light, you have a condition known as photic sneezing. Physicians aren't sure why light makes some people sneeze. An estimated 30 percent of the population is thought to suffer from photic sneezing. The condition is not considered dangerous: In fact, some doctors say that glancing quickly at a bright light may be a good way to trigger a sneeze on those occasions when you feel one coming on but can't quite manage to release it.

Is it all right to suppress a sneeze? Sneezes do seem to sneak up on us at the worst possible moments—during a concert, a lecture, or when we're just about to say, "I do." If you hold it in, the resulting implosion could potentially damage small bones in your nose and face or even rupture an eardrum.

So don't be embarrassed. Take a tissue and say, "Ahh-choo." Then blow your nose and say, "I do."

Q Why does water make your skin pruned?

A When you spend enough time in water, the skin on your feet and hands gets wrinkled, or "pruned." No, it doesn't age you: If it did, there would be a lot of filthy people around, clinging to their youth. After you get out of water, your skin eventually returns to normal. The reason for this has to do with how our skin is composed.

Skin is made up of three layers. The deepest layer is subcutaneous tissue that includes fat, nerves, and connective tissue. The second layer is dermis, where you can find your sweat glands, hair roots, nerves, and blood vessels. The top layer (the wrinkle-maker) is the epidermis. The surface—or top outer layer—of the epidermis is made of dead keratin cells. Keratin, which is also part of finger-nails, is there to protect the rest of the skin. Your hands and feet have the thickest layer of keratin; since you use these appendages all the time, they need to have an extra protective coating. We couldn't do much if the skin on our hands and feet was as thin as that on our eyelids.

So what happens when you go for a swim or soak in the tub? The keratin absorbs a lot of water. In order to make room for it all, wrinkles form and the skin plumps. Why wrinkling as opposed to just plain ol' swelling? Because the top layer is connected to the other layers of skin, but in an uneven manner. The bottom layers of skin are more waterproof than the top layer, so the water has to sit there for a while before it can be absorbed. Water that is not absorbed by the skin will evaporate, which returns your skin to normal.

The rest of your skin doesn't have such a thick layer of keratin, so it isn't as wrinkle-prone. The rest of your body also has hair, at the base of which are glands that secrete an oil called sebum. The sebum coats the hair follicles. We all know how oil and water react—the skin does not absorb as much water on your non-hand and non-feet skin. Therefore, the rest of you stays wrinkle-free.

Q Why does hair grow in all the wrong places when you age?

A Let's be honest: The older we get, the prettier we ain't. In addition to the sagging and the wrinkles, an ignominious side effect of aging is the dense thicket of hair that erupts from the ears, nose, and just about anywhere else you don't want it. While you have no choice but to accept the grim destiny of old age, you can at least know what cruel twist of anatomical fate produces this phenomenon.

Whether you are a man or woman, the culprit appears to be female hormones. And take notice of the word "appears." You should know up front that afflictions such as cancer and diabetes, not excessive nose hair, are what tend to get most of the medical attention and research funding. Consequently, the explanation that follows is mostly conjecture.

Both men and women produce female hormones such as estrogen. These hormones restrict the growth of body hair and counteract male-type hormones such as testosterone (which are also present in both men and women), which trigger the growth of body hair. When you're younger, the male and female hormones maintain the balance they should. As you get older, production of the female hormones slows down. In other words, the male-female hormonal balance gets out of whack, and you begin to look like a Yeti.

But it isn't all doom and gloom for old-timers: They get cheap movie tickets and can force people to sit through their long, rambling stories.

Q Why does a person get goose bumps?

A We've all had the feeling: You get cold or are overwhelmed with a sense of awe, perhaps while watching a fireworks display or a soap opera, and little bumps suddenly appear on your arms, legs, or neck. These are goose bumps, nature's way of saying, "Hey, I'm cold," "I'm f-f-frightened," or "Wow, I can't believe that just happened."

Goose bumps are one of mankind's evolutionary leftovers—bodily structures and functions that were useful at one time in distant prehistory but are now basically pointless, like the appendix. Back when people had more hair, according to one common theory, goose bumps would raise that hair up and trap warm air against the skin to help warm it. Nowadays, only Robin Williams would benefit from this phenomenon.

Goose bumps are an involuntary reflex set off by the sympathetic nervous system. The nerves of the skin cause the little muscles that surround the hair follicles to contract—and you break out in tiny bumps. They're called "goose bumps" because of the way a bird's skin looks when plucked. The term is actually a relatively recent addition to the vernacular—it didn't land a spot in the dictionary until 1933—but "gooseflesh" was used to describe this skin-crawling sensation as far back as the early eighteen hundreds.

And humans aren't the only animals who get it. If you've ever seen a startled cat, you'll notice that the cat's tail appears to become much larger and "poofs" out. This is caused by a reflex that's much like our own—but the cat actually has enough hair for goose bumps to be useful. Many animals appear larger when their hairs stand at attention, which helps to intimidate predators and rivals. And since we also get goose bumps when we feel intense fear or some other extreme emotion, it might have been used to the same effect by our evolutionary ancestors.

Now, though, they are used to help describe a feeling—as in, "It gave me goose bumps"—and not least of all, to name successful scary-book franchises.

Q Why do you get "brain freeze" after eating or drinking something cold?

A We're all familiar with "brain freeze," the searing head pain that occurs after a rapid ingestion of cold liquid or food. It's the body's way of saying, "Slow down, Hoss. You don't have to finish that entire gallon of ice cream in two spoonfuls." One can't help but wonder what miracle of evolution produced such an effective safety measure.

There aren't a lot of concrete answers—scientists aren't even sure what causes a normal headache—but here's what we know: The headache associated with brain freeze lasts about thirty to sixty seconds and can occur in just about any region of the cranium (front, sides, back, top). Brain freeze is clinically known as a "referred" pain because while the stimulus is in the mouth or throat, the pain manifests itself in what a layman might describe as the brain. Brain freeze is much more likely to occur in hot weather than cold, and it usually peaks after about ten seconds.

Finally, brain freezes are not fatal. Why is this last bit important? You see, gentle reader, researchers spend the bulk of their time getting to the bottom of medical issues like cancer and heart disease, so a detailed analysis of cold-stimulus headaches will just have to wait until those other mysteries are solved.

Nevertheless, there is no shortage of theories about brain freeze. The prevailing one is that brain freeze is caused by vascular changes. "Vascular" is just a fancy way of describing the systems that ship fluids such as blood around your body. The coldness of, say, ice cream overstimulates the trigeminal nerve—which carries sensory information from the face, teeth, and tongue to the brain—causing the arteries that lead to the brain to contract.

This means there is less oxygen-rich blood flowing to your head. To compensate, the blood vessels in the brain expand to let more blood through. The expansion and contraction of these blood vessels is what many researchers believe causes headaches such as brain freeze.

Brain freeze certainly serves the purpose the body intends. Few of us can continue gorging on ice cream while experiencing its wrath. If only the body had similar defenses for other poor choices—maybe a debilitating leg cramp before you have unprotected sex, or an uncontrollable sneezing fit before you buy a Michael Bolton album.

Q Why does scratching relieve itching?

A The urge to scratch is ancient and universal. Who among us has not sighed with relieved satisfaction as a set of nails repeatedly raked down our backs? On the surface, the call-and-response relationship of the itch and the scratch is relatively simple, but there have been some recent scientific discoveries that show there's more to it than just irritation and relief.

Scratching is first and foremost a diversionary tactic. By scratching, you're causing yourself a small amount of pain. This pain diverts the brain's attention away from the itch for a short time. As the pain fades, the itch returns. This is why hospital patients who are dosed with painkillers often report feeling intense itching sensations: You can't effectively scratch an itch if you can't feel any pain.

Most itches are caused by skin irritation. They're the body's way of saying that something's not right. When a bug lands on you, for example, your skin registers an itchy sensation so that you'll scratch the itch and shoo the bug away before it bites you. Irritation also can come from dry skin or harsh enzymes that are absorbed by the skin, as is the case with mosquito bites or poison ivy.

On the other hand, chronic itch—a common disorder that disrupts sleep and can cause embarrassing inflammations of the skin—is not caused by a single external irritant: Its causes are usually internal, stemming from disease or from psychological instability.

While scientists may not know for sure why some itches occur, a study conducted by a dermatologist at Wake Forest University Baptist Medical Center and published in January 2008 has gone a long way toward explaining why scratching brings on such intense relief. By studying the brain's reaction to scratching, scientists have determined that the action itself causes decreased activity in areas of the brain devoted to bad memories and unpleasant sensations. So scratching can be a kind of therapy; if an itch is purely psychological, then scratching provides a measure of mental relief.

As good as it might feel, scratching is highly discouraged by dermatologists because it can damage the skin. They recommend cold creams and antihistamine drugs to take care of the itches caused by physical irritants. And if you need psychological relief, you can always try asking a therapist to apply the cream for you.

Chapter Seven

FOOD AND DRINK

Q Can Coca-Cola burn a hole in your stomach?

A The world's most famous soft drink has been the subject of seemingly countless urban legends. One suggests that Coca-Cola can cause death from carbon dioxide poisoning, another says that it dissolves teeth, and still another posits that it makes an effective spermicide.

The topic here is whether Coke can burn a hole in your stomach. The answer is, quite simply, no. Your stomach is designed to withstand punishment—it's the Rocky Balboa of internal organs—and it can handle a lot worse than what little old Coca-Cola throws at it.

Your stomach takes every culinary delight that you consume and prepares it for the body to use as fuel. It breaks down food using hydrochloric acid—a substance that, in its industrial form, is used to process steel and leather, make household cleaning products, and even aid in oil drilling in the North Sea. Since this acid is highly corrosive, a mucus is secreted to protect the stomach lining.

The strength of an acid is measured on a pH scale that ranges from zero to fourteen. A pH level of seven is considered neutral; any substance with a pH level of less than seven is acidic. Where does your stomach's hydrochloric acid fall on the pH scale? Its pH level is one, meaning that it is among the most potent acidsin existence. Coca-Cola contains phosphoric acid, a substance with a pH level of about 2.5. Phosphoric acid, then, is less potent than what is already inside you. In other words, Coca-Cola isn't going to burn a hole in your stomach.

Still, there are some reasons to hesitate before you take the pause that refreshes. Coca-Cola contains the stimulant caffeine. (There is a caffeine-free Coca-Cola, but we're talking about the original version.) The stomach reacts to stimulants by creating more acid, which isn't an issue when the stomach is working well. But when the stomach contains ulcer-causing bacteria called *Helicobacter pylori,* the production of extra acid can exacerbate the problem. Further, people with gastroesophageal reflux disease (GERD) should avoid caffeinated drinks. And finally, phosphoric acid has been linked to osteoporosis.

But under ordinary circumstances, a big swig of Coca-Cola isn't going to harm your stomach, or any other part of your body. Enjoy. Just don't pour any on raw pork. Apparently, that will cause worms to crawl out of the meat.

Q What's the unhealthiest dish ever concocted?

A You probably wanted us to conduct serious research into this one—maybe some double-blind studies, perhaps a bunch of empirical data. That would be neat. But, to paraphrase *Animal House*'s Otter when he's contemplating an assault on the entire Faber College Greek system, it would take years and cost millions of lives. Besides, a stupendous effort is unnecessary when there's the Hamdog.

The Hamdog was created several years ago by a bar owner in Decatur, Georgia. It starts as a hot dog wrapped in a hamburger patty. It's deep-fried, smothered in chili, cheese, and onions, and served on a hoagie bun. Oh, by the way, it's topped with a fried egg and a pile of French fries. The same guy invented the Luther Burger, a bacon cheeseburger served on a bun fashioned from a Krispy Kreme doughnut. Luckily for humanity, the bar has since closed.

A report on the Hamdog said the burger and hot dog alone comprise eighty-five grams of fat—well above the average person's recommended daily intake of sixty-five grams. Factor in its other ingredients and consider the fat that's absorbed in the frying process, and the Hamdog might deliver a week's worth of dietary fat—much of it the bad kind. And that's not even considering its cured-meat chemicals and other bad molecules.

The bottom line? The Hamdog packs enough artery-hardening punch to earn the "unhealthiest" prize in our book, particularly since we're suddenly too queasy to think of an alternative.

Q Whiskey is whiskey, right?

A Yeah, like cars are cars. Lamborghini or Saturn, what's the diff?

The United States alone produces more than five hundred brands of whiskey, ranging in style from the mellow bourbons of Kentucky to the bracing Pennsylvania ryes that were enjoyed by our colonial forefathers. Other distinctive whiskies are crafted with care in Canada, Ireland, and Scotland—as well as in newer distilleries in Japan, Wales, and India. There are whiskies that are made from almost every conceivable mixture of corn, rye, and barley, and the particular recipe that is used for any given style of the spirit—along with other nuances, like the aging process and the malting technique—imparts a unique flavor that can create great differences between one whiskey and the next.

To get a sense of the extent of these differences, just look at the spelling. Canadian and Scottish distilleries make *whisky*—no e—while American and Irish distillers refer to their own products as *whiskey*. If they can't even agree on how to spell it, can *whiskey* and *whisky* really be interchangeable?

Still, there are fundamental similarities between all whiskies. Regardless of the variety, the whiskey-making process involves the same basic steps: First, the grain is soaked until it begins to sprout, and then is dried—a process called malting. The malt is ground, mixed with water, and heated—a process called mashing. Yeast is added to the mash, which allows the mixture to ferment. This produces a liquid that's similar to beer (though without the hops), which is then distilled, or evaporated and condensed—this eliminates impurities and increases the alcohol content dramatically. After distilling comes the last step: aging in wooden barrels. (And by the way, the age of a whiskey refers only to how long it was in the barrel, not how long it was in the bottle.)

But every step has variations. In Ireland, for example, whiskey-makers often blend barley with other grains and age their liquor at least three years. In Scotland, the sprouted barley is usually dried using peat for fuel—yes, that's decaying plant matter that's dredged up from a bog and dried—which gives Scotch whisky a smoky, swampy flavor.

In Canada, blended whiskies are popular. These are made by blending the distilled products of aromatic combinations of various grains (especially rye) with flavorless but powerful neutral spirits: This process gives Canadian whiskies a smoothness that is enhanced by being aged in charred oak barrels. Charred oak also plays a role in America's favorite whiskey: bourbon. Named for Bourbon County, Kentucky, the malt must be at least 51 percent corn and mixed (usually) with barley and rye. It's then aged—by law—in new charred oak barrels for at least two years.

Then there's rye whiskey, which is made primarily from the grain that's used in dark pumpernickel bread. Its sharp, spicy taste helped fuel the American Revolution; George Washington himself distilled it, sold it, and drank it at Mount Vernon.

All these spirits can be sipped at room temperature by themselves ("neat"), over ice, or with water or soda. With hundreds of brands to taste, you could spend the rest of your life cultivating a connoisseur's appreciation of whiskey.

Q What's so American about apple pie?

A Apple pie is so beloved in America that it's a cultural icon right up there with hot dogs, baseball, and Chevrolet. Funny thing is, the double-crust pastry that is filled with fruit and seasoned with cinnamon wasn't even invented in the United States.

Was that your dessert fork dropping to the floor? Think about it: Apples aren't indigenous to the United States—they were brought here by English colonists. Remember the story of John Chapman, a.k.a. Johnny Appleseed? Truth be told, apple pies were being baked long before settlers arrived on North American shores. In fact, pies have been around in one form or another since the ancient Egyptians first created the pastry crust. The Greeks and Romans, for example, made main-dish pies filled with meat.

According to the American Pie Council, the first fruit-filled pies or tarts (called "pasties") were likely created in the fifteen hundreds. In the Tudor and Stuart eras, English pies were made with cherries, pears, quinces, and—yes—apples.

So okay, apple pie isn't innately American. It came here with the first settlers. But gosh darn if we didn't perfect it and make it all our own. You see, the early English apple pies were usually made without sugar. And the crusts were often tough and inedible, used more for holding the filling together than for eating.

According to *The Oxford Encyclopedia of Food and Drink in America,* the typical American pie evolved to be made with uncooked apples, fat, sugar, and sweet spices. Now we're talking! No wonder the phrase "as American as apple pie" came to be.

Whether you like your apple pie baked in a paper bag, à la mode, or topped with a slice of cheddar cheese, we took someone else's recipe and turned it into a completely American experience. Heck, apple pie is even on the menu at McDonald's. That's about as American as it gets.

Q Why is coffee called "joe"?

A With the exploding popularity of gourmet coffee drinks in recent years and the vast number of specialty, fair-trade, and organic coffee purveyors now dominating the market, it's sometimes a challenge to find a joint that serves up plain old coffee. And when you do stumble upon such a place, asking for a "cuppa joe" is more likely to be met with a blank stare than a cup of coffee (unless the barista is a fan of old, hard-boiled detective movies). Yet for much of the twentieth century, coffee was indeed referred to as joe.

Why "joe"? Why not Bob? Fred? Orville? There are a number of prevailing theories as to why coffee is referred to as joe. The first, and the one promoted by the United States Navy, holds that in 1913, new Navy Secretary Josephus Daniels abolished the policy of allowing sailors to drink alcohol at mess. In false praise, American sailors began referring to coffee—now the most powerful beverage available to them—as a "cup of joe." However, most etymologists discard this theory, pointing out that the first time that the phrase "cup of joe" appeared in print was in 1930, and a seventeen-year gap between the first colloquial use and the first recorded use is virtually unheard of.

A second explanation is only partly military in origin. The term "joe" long referred both to an average American and to an American soldier (think G.I. Joe), and because coffee is both the average man's drink of choice and a primary staple of a soldier's rations, coffee became associated with the name Joe. This makes sense, right?

The least interesting theory (but the one that's most likely correct, according to some etymologists) suggests that "joe" is a bastardization of Java, the island that for a long time was the primary source of coffee to North America. Of course, those folk pronouncing Java as "joe" might have been drinking something a lot stronger than joe. Jack, perhaps.

Q Why doesn't bubble gum dissolve in your mouth?

A Gum manufacturers try to keep their recipes top secret, but the Wrigley Company acknowledges that most gum is made from four basic components: sweeteners, softeners, flavorings, and gum base.

Those first three categories include ingredients such as sugar, corn syrup, aspartame, glycerin, vegetable oil, and natural and artificial flavorings such as spearmint or cotton candy. These ingredients are all soluble, meaning your saliva will dissolve them as you chew.

This is where the fourth component—gum base—comes in. The gum base stands up to your saliva and maintains its integrity as you grind it between your teeth or blow it into a bubble. Historically, gum base was tapped from natural sources like sorva, jelutong, and chicle, the sap from sapodilla trees.

Today, those natural sources run pretty scarce, so scientists have developed synthetic gum-base materials. Natural or unnatural, gum base does not disintegrate in your mouth.

Why? Because it's essentially a form of rubber. Think of chewing on a rubber band, super ball, pencil eraser, or car tire. None of these will dissolve in your mouth either. (Please, take our word on this!)

Of course, a piece of bubble gum tastes a lot better than an old yellow raincoat, and it's much easier to chew. This is because the rubber in gum base is softer and smoother than normal rubber, and it unites the other, more delicious ingredients. When you chew on it, the flavors of "gushing grape" and "strawberry splash" are released into your mouth, though they don't last long.

And if you swallow a wad of chewing gum? It will come out your other end in one whole piece. And it won't take seven years to digest, as urban legend suggests. It'll run through your system in just a few days.

Q What's the best way to treat a hangover?

A Let's hope that you are not afflicted now, since reading—as well as moving, breathing, and maintaining consciousness—is too painful an activity to pursue while in the throes of veisalgia, the medical term for hangover. And frankly, the best time to treat a hangover is before it even starts, so if your pulse is already pounding in your temples and your stomach is doing back flips, you've missed your best chance to nip it in the bud. Still, feel free to read on (if you can bear it) for some sage advice that can make the morning after that next Christmas party a little more pleasant.

A great deal of a hangover's agony is due to simple dehydration. Alcohol sucks the water out of you, so the smartest thing you can do while imbibing is to have one glass of water for each cocktail. Drink some more water before you stumble into bed and put a nice big bottle of H_2O on the nightstand to drink when you wake. Those frequent trips to the bathroom will totally pay off.

Another pre-hangover hint: Stick with clear liquor. Research shows that transparent tipples like vodka and gin are the best bets. Why?

Darker liquors have more congeners in them. Congeners are by-products of fermentation; as your body processes them, it can produce formaldehyde, which (given formaldehyde's utility as an embalming fluid) helps to explain why you wake up the next morning feeling half dead.

But sometimes all the foresight in the world won't prevent a hangover. So what can you do about it? We recommend a simple course of action:

Drink lots of fluids—water, fruit juice, or maybe even a bottle of your favorite sports drink. If you feel extremely dehydrated, avoid coffee and other caffeinated drinks because they'll only dry you out more. Down a pain reliever if you think your stomach can take it (and if your stomach isn't ready yet, you'll probably also want to avoid acidic drinks like orange, grapefruit, and tomato juices). Most importantly, crawl back into bed: More sleep will do wonders. If you can't sleep, take a warm shower to improve your circulation and try some bland food like crackers, bananas, or toast. Once you're up, light exercise can help put the pain behind you.

One more thing—and repeat it over and over: "I promise never to drink this much again."

Q Why do Wint-O-Green Life Savers spark when bitten in the dark?

A Looking to create some sparks on your next date? Pop a Wint-O-Green Life Saver into your mouth before going in for a kiss. With one bite, you'll have impeccably fresh breath—and your own mini light show.

Ah, the fireworks of young love! And isn't it romantic that what's going on here is quite literally the science of attraction? The blue-white sparks of Wint-O-Green Life Savers are created through a process called triboluminescence, or light generated though friction.

Here's how it works: When the Life Saver is bitten, the sugar crystals in the candy break into fragments that are positively and negatively charged. These charges tend to retreat to opposite sides, but just as they're being pushed away from each other, they decide that they want to get back together. To do this, they jump across the air and back into each other's arms—making, in essence, tiny lightning bolts.

Wint-O-Green Life Savers aren't the only candies that create sparks of triboluminescence. In fact, most hard, sugary candies—and even plain old sugar cubes—produce a glow of ultraviolet light when cracked. But most of the time, the light is too faint to be seen. Why do Wint-O-Green Life Savers produce a greater amount of visible light? The oil of wintergreen flavoring in the candy (methyl salicylate) is naturally fluorescent. The fluorescent oil converts nearly invisible ultraviolet light into a visible bright blue light, which adds to the triboluminescent effect.

To try this at home, find a dark room and bring a mirror. If you happen to be in the company of a date, here's a last bit of advice: Make sure this is the only time you chew with your mouth open.

Q Who determines the serving size on a food product container?

A When it comes to food portions, many health-conscious consumers follow the figures that have been established by the U.S. Department of Agriculture (USDA). But these consumers don't realize that the USDA only defines standard serving sizes for "guidance" and "prevention" purposes: The Food and Drug

Administration (FDA) is the outfit that conjures the serving sizes that are listed on food products.

The USDA Food Guide Pyramid helps the FDA determine the serving size on, say, the box of mouthwatering garlic croutons that will likely be emptied in one sitting. Serving sizes are based on FDA-established lists of the amounts of food an average American eats during a typical meal. The USDA also has serving sizes in its Food Guide Pyramid, but these figures are often at odds with the FDA's.

If you're a little confused, you're not alone—most Americans don't realize that the USDA serving sizes differ from those of the FDA. This discrepancy occurs because the figures have separate purposes. The USDA serving size is a unit that's designed to be easy to remember and convenient to use when planning a meal. An FDA food-label serving is supposed to make it simple for consumers to compare the nutritional values of similar items, even if it's less handy as a measure of exactly what they're eating.

The following food items exemplify the differences in standard serving sizes between the FDA and the USDA:

Item	USDA	FDA
Beer	12 ounces	8 ounces
White bread	1 ounce	1.8 ounces
Cooked pasta	1/2 cup	1 cup

So who really determines the serving sizes of food products? The FDA, with a little help from its friend, the USDA.

Q Why do doughnuts have holes?

A The saga of how doughnuts came to have holes is a bit of a mystery; perhaps a police detective is needed to solve it. What cop wouldn't want to pore over mountains of evidence that involves doughnuts?

The origin of doughnuts most likely can be traced to Northern Europe during medieval times. Called *olykoeks* ("oily cakes"), the pastries came to America with the Pilgrims, who had picked up the recipe in Holland, their first refuge from England, which they abandoned for America in the early sixteen hundreds. The dough in the middle of these pastries rarely got cooked, so that area often was filled with apples, prunes, or raisins.

By the mid-eighteen hundreds, the pastries were being made with a hole in the middle—and this is where the plot thickens. Two stories about the origin of the hole involve Hanson Crockett Gregory, a sea captain from Rockport, Maine. One says that he poked out the middle of one of his wife's homemade doughnuts by plunging it into a spoke on the ship's wheel. That eliminated the uncooked middle, and it enabled Gregory to eat and keep his boat at an even keel at the same time.

A second story—this one slightly more plausible—involves Gregory eating doughnuts with other crew members. Tired of the raw dough in the middle, he took a tin off the ship's pepper box and used it to push out the middle, leaving only the cooked edges. He tasted it and exclaimed that it was the best doughnut he had ever eaten. Years later, in 1916, Gregory recounted this story in the *Washington Post*.

There is no real proof that backs up either account involving Gregory, but this much is certain: A plaque commemorating his culinary claim stands at the house in Maine where he lived. And perhaps not coincidentally, doughnuts did indeed have holes by the mid-eighteen hundreds, making them easier to cook and improving their taste.

Once they started coming with holes in them, doughnuts soared in popularity. During WWI, the French gave doughnuts to American soldiers to remind them of home. In the 1920s, doughnuts were the snack of choice in movie theaters. At the 1934 World's Fair in Chicago, they were called, "The food hit of the Century of Progress." Cops all over America couldn't agree more.

Q Why did we start mixing other stuff with hard liquor?

A Yankee ingenuity? Or maybe it was our sweet tooth. While straight booze was historically the beverage of the masses, mixed drinks with lots of sugar added were reserved for wealthy landowners.

In 1806, a Hudson, New York, newspaper defined a cocktail as stimulating liquor combined with sugar, spirits of any sort, bitters, and water. This was one of the first recorded uses of the word "cocktail" in print. No one can be sure where the word originated, though there are many anecdotes.

Colonial Americans drank beer, wine, cider, and rum, and sometimes mixed rum into punch. By the late seventeen hundreds, visitors to the United States observed that Americans liked to start the day with a "sling": a drink of strong spirits, sugar, and bitters or herbs. The mint julep was a sling. Men often downed several slings before lunchtime.

Cocktails were mentioned by early American writers, including Washington Irving and James Fenimore Cooper, author of *Last of the Mohicans.* A cocktail recipe book appeared in the 1860s. The first martini recipe was printed in 1884, though the ingredients were not what we'd put into a martini today—early martinis were sweet, not dry.

Sweet alcoholic drinks were mixed in the home, at parties, and sometimes in fine hotels. Saloons did not serve them: They sold only straight liquor and beer, not cocktails, until sometime in the 1880s. Mixed drinks then became so popular that saloon owners became mixologists, and cocktails went on to enjoy a golden age of innovation.

Prohibition ended this golden age in 1920. Selling alcohol was suddenly illegal, so the trade moved underground. This hardly stopped consumption, though.

Adding soft drinks or milk stretched the precious bootlegged whiskey and masked the vile taste of bathtub gin. Cocktails remained in high demand and were sold in speakeasies during Prohibition; ever since, they've been hawked at bars, clubs, and restaurants.

Journalist H. L. Mencken contended that the cocktail is "the greatest of all the contributions of the American way of life to the salvation of humanity." No telling how many "contributions" he had enjoyed on the night he wrote that.

Q Why does bottled water have a "best if used by" date?

A In the United States, bottled water is considered a packaged food. Thus, it is regulated by the U.S. Food and Drug Administration (FDA). According to the FDA's Current Good Manufacturing Practices (CGMP), all bottled water must be sampled, analyzed, and found to be safe and sanitary. CGMP regulations also specify proper bottling procedures, record keeping, and plant and equipment design.

And that's not all. Bottled water must adhere to state regulations, and bottled-water producers that are members of the International Bottled Water Association must follow that trade organization's code, which runs a stupefying thirty pages. The different ways that bottled water can be described on the label include: spring water, purified water, mineral water, distilled water, drinking water, and artesian water. According to the FDA, carbonated water, seltzer water, soda water, sparkling water, and tonic water are soft drinks, so they are not regulated as bottled water.

What does all of this have to do with the "best if used by" date on many of the bottles of water that are consumed in the United States? Plenty. Bottled water that meets FDA requirements has an indefinite shelf life, according to the agency. Therefore, the FDA does not require bottlers to list a "best if used by" date on approved water, nor does it require an expiration date.

With bottled water, there really is no difference between an expiration date and a "best if used by" date. Major bottled water companies such as Evian, Poland Spring, Aquafina, and Perrier, to name some, voluntarily place expiration dates on their containers as a courtesy to customers. The water is still safe to drink after the listed date if the container has retained its seal, according to a Poland Spring spokesperson, but it could exhibit off-flavors or odors if it has not been stored properly. The typical expiration date is two years from the packaging date. Dasani, a Coca-Cola brand, stamps a one-year expiration date on its water. The popular Fiji brand uses a "best if used by" date.

The FDA Center for Food Safety and Applied Nutrition defines "best if used by" as the deadline for consuming a food to assure the best flavor and quality. But if you store your unopened bottled water in a cool place, that date might never truly arrive.

Q Why does sourdough bread taste better in San Francisco?

A The secret is in the air. A strain of wild microorganisms called *Lactobacillus sanfrancisco* that flourish in San Francisco's mild, damp climate lends a unique tangy flavor to the bread during the leavening process. Sourdough bakers in other locales can't achieve the same tangy flavor without *Lactobacillus sanfrancisco*.

To make sourdough bread, San Francisco bakers start by mixing flour and water. The mixture attracts yeasts, *Lactobacillus sanfrancisco,* and other bacteria from the air. The microorganisms feed on the flour and multiply. At the same time, the yeasts emit carbon dioxide, which causes the dough to rise, and the bacteria produce vinegar and lactic acid. The vinegar and lactic acid also contribute to the unique flavor of San Francisco sourdough.

Sourdough bread has been around since 1500 BC, when the Egyptians first discovered leavening agents. It became a true taste treat when it arrived in San Francisco in the mid-nineteenth century, at around the time of the California Gold Rush. San Francisco's first sourdough bakers, the Boudin family, opened up shop in 1849, and soon dozens of other bakeries cropped up, including Parisian, Toscana, and Colombo.

If you don't live in San Francisco, don't fret—you can still enjoy the taste of San Francisco sourdough bread at home. Pure cultures of *Lactobacillus sanfrancisco* are freeze-dried and supplied to bakeries around the world.

Q Why is red wine served at room temperature and white wine chilled?

A Would you enjoy lukewarm lemonade or not-so-hot hot chocolate? Didn't think so.

Researchers at Belgium's Katholieke Universiteit Leuven have discovered that our taste buds perceive flavors differently at different temperatures. Specifically, the warmer the food or beverage in your mouth is, the stronger the electric flavor signal that travel from your taste receptors to your brain are. This can be a good or a bad thing, depending on what you're eating or drinking. For example, frozen ice cream tastes sweeter as it melts on your tongue, but a beer tastes bitter after it's gotten warm in the sun.

But back to the grape juice. The whole point of chilling (or not chilling) a wine is to serve it at a temperature at which our taste buds will be most tantalized by it. Cold makes white wines less sweet and more refreshingly crisp and acidic, and helps champagnes and sparklers retain their bubbles long after you've popped the cork. Reds tend to be a bit more tannic (biting) than whites, so a little warmth goes a long way in making them taste more fruity and aromatic.

Wine snobs (okay, "wine experts") will tell you that the proper serving temperature is crucial to bringing out a wine's optimal flavor, aroma, and structure (how it feels on your tongue). Frankly, some of these people can get a little obsessed. They will spout out general rules such as these: Sparkling wine must be served at forty-eight degrees Fahrenheit, white wine at fifty-three degrees Fahrenheit, rosé wine at fifty-one degrees Fahrenheit, and red wine at sixty-two degrees Fahrenheit.

The experts have the best intentions. After all, serving a wine too warm or too cold can negatively affect its flavor. A white that's overly frigid can taste . . . well, tasteless. And a red that's too toasty can seem too alcoholic, even vinegary.

What's a wine drinker without a fancy wine cellar to do? First of all, don't lose any sleep over the precise optimal serving temperature for your favorite Two-Buck Chuck. Just follow this super-simple rule of thumb from wine educator Mark Oldman (*Oldman's Guide to Outsmarting Wine*): Fifteen minutes before serving time, take white wines out of the fridge and pop the red ones in.

Chapter Eight

WEIRD SCIENCE AND TECHNOLOGY

Q What's the smelliest thing on earth?

A Perhaps the skunk gets a bad rap. When someone wants to describe an object—or perhaps an acquaintance—as stinking up the place, the poor skunk is invariably used as the reference point.

It's true that the *Guinness Book of World Records* lists butyl sele-no-mercaptan, an ingredient in the skunk's defense mechanism, among the worst-smelling chemicals in nature. But according to scientists and laboratory tests in various parts of the world, there are far fouler odors than a skunk's spray. Some of the most offen-sive nose-wrinklers are man-made. Dr. Anne Marie Helmenstine, writing in *Your Guide to Chemistry,* suggests that a couple of molecular compounds—which were invented specifically to be incredibly awful—could top the list.

One is named Who-Me? This sulfur-based chemical requires five ingredients to produce a stench comparable to that of a rotting carcass. Who-Me? was created during World War II so that French resistance fighters could humiliate German soldiers by making them stink to high heaven. The stuff proved almost as awful for its handlers, who found it difficult to apply so that they, too, didn't wind up smelling like dead flesh.

For commercial craziness, consider the second compound cited by Helmenstine. American chemists developed a combination of eight molecules in an effort to re-create the smell of human feces. Why? To test the effectiveness of commercially produced air fresheners and deodorizers. Ever imaginative, the chemists named their compound U.S. Government Standard Bathroom Malodor.

For many people, cheese comes to mind when thinking of man-made smells that make the eyes water. There is, in fact, an official smelliest cheese—a French delight called Vieux Boulogne. Constructed from cow's milk by Philippe Olivier, Vieux Boulogne was judged the world's smelliest cheese by nineteen members of a human olfactory panel, plus an electronic nose developed at Cranfield University in England. London's *Guardian* newspaper insisted that Vieux Boulogne gave off an aroma of "barnyard dung" from a distance of fifty meters.

A skunk would have a hard time matching that, and Pepe Le Pew might even take a backseat to the Bombardier beetle. This insect is armed with two chemicals, hydroquinone and hydrogen peroxide.

When it feels threatened, the chemicals combine with an enzyme that heats the mixture. The creature then shoots a boiling, stinky liquid and gas from its rear. Humans unfortunate enough to have endured the experience claim that there's nothing worse.

No less a luminary than nineteenth-century naturalist Charles Darwin allegedly suffered both the smell and sting of the Bombardier beetle's spray when, during a beetle-collecting expedition, he put one in his mouth to free up a hand. Consider Darwin a genius if you like, but his common sense left something to be desired.

Q Can a human voice really shatter a glass?

A You're not likely to do it accidentally, even if you do spend a lot of time yelling at your tableware, but it's definitely possible.

First, a few words about air, space, and sound. The word "air" probably makes you think of nothingness—empty space. But the air we breathe is actually a fluid—a gas—in which we are immersed. And the sounds that we hear are actually vibrations that travel through this fluid like waves.

Your vocal cords are machines for creating these waves. When you speak, sing, freestyle beat-box, etc., air from your lungs rushes past your vocal cords, and those two taut membranes vibrate. First, the outrushing air makes your vocal cords flex outward, pushing out a wave of increased air pressure; then they rebound inward, creating a wave of decreasing air pressure.

When your vocal cords vibrate, they're moving in and out incredibly quickly to create waves of air pressure fluctuation, or sound. The sound's pitch is determined in part by how rapidly your vocal cords are vibrating—in other words, the *frequency* of the air pressure fluctuation. The sound's volume is determined by the force of each fluctuation, or the wave's amplitude.

Sound waves travel through the fluid air and vibrate against anything they encounter. For example, sound waves rapidly move your eardrums back and forth, which is how you hear. And if a sound is loud enough, its waves can have other effects. If you've ever been at a stop light behind a car with a booming audio system in the back, you may have noticed that the trunk looks like it's shuddering under the stress of those sound waves. But the auditory assault of even the loudest stereo isn't enough to break the car's windows, so how can the sound waves of a human voice shatter glass?

It has to do with frequency and resonance. The structure and composition of an object determine exactly how it will vibrate—this is known as its natural frequency. Think of a tuning fork that vibrates in just the right way to make a particular note, no matter how you hit it. You get an extra vibration boost—a resonant sound wave—when you produce a sound wave with a frequency that lines up with the object's natural vibration frequency. It's like pushing a kid on a swing—when he's moving away from you, you push him to add an extra boost. Every time you do this, the arc of the swing increases, and the kid reaches higher and higher.

In the same way, just when an object is already vibrating to the left, the resonant sound wave pushes it to the left; just when it's vibrating to the right, the resonant sound wave pushes it to the right. The amplitude steadily increases, and the object vibrates more rapidly. A crystal glass has above-average natural resonance and is fragile, so the right tone can create enough vibration to shatter it.

To break a glass with your voice, you have to do two things:

• Hit the note that has the strongest resonant frequency for the glass. This is called the fundamental frequency, or the natural frequency mentioned earlier.

• Produce a sound with enough amplitude to vibrate the glass violently. In other words, you have to be loud.

An untrained singer can accomplish this with an amplifier providing a boost. But you need a skilled singer with strong lungs to do it unassisted. Many have claimed success, but there wasn't conclusive proof until a 2005 *MythBusters* episode showed rock singer Jaime Vendera accomplishing the feat—after twenty attempts. Don't let that guy near your Waterford Crystal collection.

Q Do water towers actually hold water?

A Water towers are as iconic a part of the American landscape as Route 66 and roadside diners. As symbols of small towns across the country, water towers often take on the personality of their regions.

In Tipton, Missouri, the water tower resembles a giant eight ball. (Talk about being behind the eight ball—how would you like living behind it?) Stanton, Iowa, boasts a cup-and-saucer water tower. Several Georgia water towers look like peaches. And who can resist the charm of the enormous basketball water tower honoring the 1952 Hebron High School (student enrollment: ninety-eight) basketball team that won the Illinois state championship?

Do today's water towers provide any function beyond adding a splash of character to the landscape? In other words, do they hold water?

One might expect, in this modern age, that the water tower has run its course as a useful device and is now strictly ornamental. It seems somewhat primitive, after all, for an entire town's drinking water to be held in a giant globe. But one would be wrong to count out the good old water tower—or at least partly wrong. Though a water tower doesn't hold a town's entire water supply, it does contain about a day's worth, which is a pretty sizable quantity.

To understand why a water tower holds water, we need to take a look at how most municipal water systems operate. Most towns draw their water from wells, rivers, lakes, or other bodies of water. The water is usually pumped from the source to a water treatment plant, where it is cleaned and disinfected before being pumped into the main water delivery system of the municipality. Water towers are also hooked up to the delivery system; they draw water to serve as reservoirs. These reservoirs come in handy when water is in high demand (such as in the early morning, when people are getting ready for work and school) and the town's pump can't keep up by adding its supply to the flow. When demand drops, the globes fill back up.

Why do water towers have to be so high? The answer is water pressure. In order for the water in the towers to get to where it needs to go, it has to be forced. The higher the tower, the more water pressure builds up—and the stronger the pressure, the farther and faster the pipes can deliver water to surrounding areas. This is one reason why water remains available during a power outage: The pumps are down, but water towers, which use gravity and water pressure as power, keep delivering. It is also why you often see water towers perched atop the highest point in the area or on the tops of buildings in cities like New York and Chicago.

So water towers still serve a purpose, though it might not be long before they recede into history. More and more cities are going to electric pump systems to deliver their water. And that's a real shame. How can you paint a titanic "Look Up To Jesus" message (Gem, Indiana) on an electric pump?

Q What important stuff has been invented by women?

A If you think men have the market cornered on inventions, think again. It turns out that the fairer sex is responsible for some of history's most notable breakthroughs.

Women came up with ideas and specifications for such useful items as life rafts (Maria Beasley), circular saws (Tabitha Babbitt), medical syringes (Letitia Geer), and underwater lamps and telescopes (Sarah Mather). Giuliana Tesoro was a prolific inventor in the textile industry; flame-resistant fibers and permanent-press properties are among her many contributions, and the Tesoro Corporation holds more than 125 of her textile-related patents.

Not surprisingly, some better-known inventions by women are associated with the home. In 1930, for example, dietician Ruth Wakefield and her husband Kenneth were operating a tourist lodge near Boston. While mixing a batch of cookies for guests one day, Ruth discovered she had run out of baker's chocolate. In a rush to come up with something, Wakefield substituted broken pieces of Nestlé semi-sweet chocolate. She expected them to melt into the dough to create chocolate cookies; they didn't, and the surprising result was the chocolate chip cookie.

In the late 1950s, Ruth Handler drew inspiration from watching her daughter and her daughter's friends play with paper dolls. After noticing that the girls used the dolls to act out future events rather than those in the present, Handler set out to create a grown-up, three-dimensional doll. She even endowed it with breasts (though their proportions were later criticized for being unrealistic). Handler named the doll after her daughter, and the Barbie doll was introduced in 1959. Handler, incidentally, was one of the founders of the toy giant Mattel.

Of course, not all female inventors have been interested in cookies and dolls. Consider Mary Anderson. While taking a trip from Alabama to New York City just after the turn of the twentieth century, she noticed that when it rained, drivers had to open their car windows to see. Anderson invented a swinging-arm device with a rubber blade that the driver operated by using a lever. In 1903, she received a patent for what became known as the windshield wiper; by 1916, it was standard on most vehicles.

Movie actress Hedy Lamarr's invention was a matter of national security. Lamarr, born Hedwig Eva Maria Kiesler in Austria, emigrated to the United States in the 1930s. In addition to leading the glamorous life of a film star, she became a pioneer in the field of wireless communication.

Lamarr and musical composer George Anthiel developed a secret communications system to help the Allies in World War II—their method of manipulating radio frequencies was used to create unbreakable codes. The invention proved invaluable again two decades later when it was used aboard naval vessels during the Cuban Missile Crisis.

The "spread spectrum" technology that Lamarr helped to pioneer became the key component in the creation of cellular phones, fax machines, and other wireless devices. How's that for inventive?

Q Why do toilets flush backwards in Australia?

A What do you mean by backwards? Toilets in the United States, we are grateful to note, flush in a general downward direction. And given the relative popularity of Australia as a travel destination, we can only infer that the toilets there do likewise. Because if they flushed in an upward direction, nobody would want to (ahem) "go" there.

If, on the other hand, you're referring to the direction in which the water in a flushing toilet swirls, the answer gets a little more complicated—but not by much.

Our fascination with Australian plumbing is related to our awareness of something called the Coriolis force. We heard about it during our high school physical science classes, but most of us paid only enough attention to remember the term. We're not so adept at recalling the details of what it is or what it does.

The Coriolis force is named for the man who developed the concept, French scientist Gaspard-Gustave de Coriolis. He did a bunch of math that provided an answer for why weather systems spin in different directions depending on whether they're north or south of the equator. Let's eschew the elaborate equations and boil it down to this: As the earth spins on its axis, large air masses are pushed along in the direction of the rotation, and the air nearest the equator moves the fastest. That, in turn, affects the spin of cyclones. So in the Northern Hemisphere, cyclones spin counterclockwise; in the Southern Hemisphere, they spin clockwise. Spin a globe (a real globe, not something Google has created) and it's pretty easy to imagine how that motion affects the atmosphere.

Some of our less-studious peers, who are armed with dangerously little knowledge of the Coriolis force, have surmised that the rotation of the earth must also have an effect on water as it swirls down a drain. But as you've probably guessed by now, they're wrong. The Coriolis effect is only demonstrable on a huge scale over a long period of time.

Depending on what you've been eating lately, you may occasionally think that your flushes happen on a huge scale over a long period of time, but they're not large or long enough to qualify for Coriolis status. The truth is that regardless of whether you're in Australia, Austria, or Austin, Texas, the direction that your toilet flushes is dictated by the design of your toilet: Some send their water in a clockwise direction, and others send it counterclockwise.

And if you're lucky (and regular), it should all travel in the most important direction of all: down.

Q Why does El Niño upset weather patterns?

A El Niño, that problem child of climatology, has been blamed for disasters around the world: forest fires in southeast Asia, deadly floods in central Europe, tornadoes in Florida, mudslides in California, droughts in Zimbabwe, and devastating tropical storms in Central America.

What exactly is this atmospheric arch-villain, and where does it come from?

Named, ironically, for the Christ child, the scourge known as El Niño is not so much a single event as it is a predictably unpredictable combination of meteorological conditions that usually arrives in December. The disruptive patterns of El Niño appear roughly once every two to ten years, and to understand what El Niño does, you first have to consider what happens when it doesn't show up.

Ordinarily, during the closing months of the year, trade winds along the equator in the Pacific Ocean blow warm surface water westward, forming an immense warm pool northeast of Australia. At the same time, in the east, off the coast of Peru, cooler water rises to replace the warm water that has moved west. The warm pool in the west serves as a weather machine, pumping moisture into the atmosphere that generates storms all around the planet, in generally predictable patterns.

But some years, for reasons unknown to scientists, the trade winds never come. The warm pool never makes it to Australia, and the cool water never rises near Peru. Instead of occupying one spot, the weather machine spreads across a large span of the equatorial Pacific, and its unpredictable location means that the weather that it generates doesn't follow recognizable patterns. This creates a domino effect around the world, forcing a whole slew of atmospheric conditions to follow new, unusual patterns.

It doesn't end there. El Niño has an obstinate little sister, La Niña, that follows El Niño around and behaves just about as badly, but in direct opposition. As the effects of El Niño taper off, the trade winds pick up and blow even harder, pushing more warm water west than usual and pulling up an overabundance of cool water in the east. This turns all of the El Niño weather patterns inside out. Eventually, the trade winds stabilize and conditions around the world return to normal. The cycle is known to meteorologists as El Niño-Southern Oscillation, or ENSO.

It's tempting to blame specific weather events on El Niño, but the truth is that El Niño merely changes weather patterns—lots of other local conditions have to conspire to create an event like a mudslide or a hurricane. It's also tempting, in these days of heightened environmental awareness, to blame El Niño and the havoc it wreaks on global warming. But El Niños have been toying with the world's weather for at least 130,000 years, and while they've grown more frequent in recent times, that trend began some ten thousand years ago.

And as we all know from watching Fred Flintstone, driving a car in the Stone Age did not leave a carbon footprint—just a lot of harmless, three-toed footprints.

Q Why does metal spark in a microwave?

A Microwave ovens work by permeating your food with microwave radiation. That sounds a little scary, but don't worry: We're not talking about the kind of radiation that gave us the giant lizard that stomped Japan. Instead, this radiation excites the water molecules that make up a large portion of every kind of food we eat. The vibrating water molecules start to get hot, which in turn heats the food.

Simple so far, right? It gets a little trickier. Metal responds quite differently to the electromagnetic field that a microwave oven creates. Unlike water, which can absorb the microwave energy, metal *reflects* the radiation. And the energy of the electromagnetic field can also cause a charge to build up in metal—especially if the metal is thin and pointy, like the tines of a fork, the handle of a Chinese take-out box, or the decorative rim on your Young Elvis commemorative plate.

When enough of a charge builds up, all of that energy in the metal can leap joyfully through the air. We see this leap as a spark—like a small-scale bolt of lightning. These arcs of electricity are most likely to emanate from sharp edges, like the tines of a fork or the ridges of crumpled aluminum foil. A solid object with no sharp edges should be okay, because any electrical charge that develops is more likely to spread itself around evenly.

But even then, there's a danger—the metal could reflect the microwave radiation back at the magnetron tube that creates the electromagnetic field. This could damage the magnetron tube, and then you'd be stuck with a useless microwave.

So here's an equation for you: metal + microwave = really bad idea. Stick to food.

Q How close are we to teleporting, like they do in *Star Trek?*

A Closer than you think, but don't squander those frequent-flyer miles just yet. There's a reason why Captain Kirk is on TV late at night shilling for a cheap-airfare Web site and not hawking BeamMeToHawaiiScotty.com. For the foreseeable future, jet travel is still the way to go.

If, however, you're a photon and need to travel a few feet in a big hurry, teleportation is a viable option.

Photons are subatomic particles that make up beams of light. In 2002, physicists at the Australian National University were able to disassemble a beam of laser light at the subatomic level and make it reappear about three feet away. There have been advances since, including an experiment in which Austrian researchers teleported a beam of light across the Danube River in Vienna via a fiber-optic cable—the first instance of teleportation taking place outside of a laboratory.

These experiments are a far cry from dematerializing on your spaceship and materializing on the surface of a strange planet to make out with an alien who, despite her blue skin, is still pretty hot. But this research demonstrates that it is possible to transport matter in a way that bypasses space—just don't expect teleportation of significant amounts of matter to happen until scientists clear a long list of hurdles, which will take many years.

Teleportation essentially scans and dematerializes an object, turning its subatomic particles into data. The data is transferred to another location and used to recreate the object. This is not unlike the way your computer downloads a file from another computer miles away. But your body consists of trillions upon trillions of atoms, and no computer today could be relied on to crunch numbers powerfully enough to transport and precisely recreate you.

As is the case with many technological advances, the most vexing, long-lasting obstacle probably won't involve creation of the technology, but moral and ethical issues surrounding its use.

Teleportation destroys an object and recreates a facsimile somewhere else. If that object is a person, does the destruction constitute murder? And if you believe that a person has a soul, is teleportation capable of recreating a person's soul within the physical body it recreates? And should we someday cross that final frontier, if BeamMeToHawaiiScotty.com becomes a reality, do you believe that William Shatner should star in the TV commercial?

Q Why do wet things look darker than dry things?

A We're able to see because light hits objects and bounces off them onto our eyes. The more light that bounces off, the brighter the objects appear. We see colors because objects absorb some frequencies of light but reflect others; the different frequencies appear to us as different colors. Black objects absorb most frequencies and therefore appear dark, while white objects reflect most frequencies and appear bright.

Now that you've had a basic lesson on sight, let's answer the question at hand. We've established that when light hits any object, some of it is reflected back and some is absorbed. Light also can be refracted through an object; this means that it bends and flies off in a different direction, so it doesn't come back to your peepers.

Take a piece of white paper; it reflects most of the light that hits it. If someone were to spill water onto that paper, the water would be absorbed into the paper. Water bends light quite a bit. (Put a stick in clear water and seen how bent it looks.) Since more light is being refracted away from our eyes, we perceive the wet spot to be darker than the rest of the piece of paper.

Water—it may seem kind of boring, but there's a lot more to it than meets the eye.

Chapter Nine

HISTORY

Q What if a duel ended in a tie?

A Ah, the romantic days of yore, when courtly ladies rode in horse-drawn carriages and gentlemen who knew the meaning of honor slapped each other with gloves and then met at dawn to fire guns at each other. To quote poet/rocker Ray Davies, "Where have all the good times gone?"

Back in the good old days, if a gentleman felt insulted, he didn't stoop to starting a shouting match, a fistfight, or even a flame war on an Internet discussion board. Instead, he had recourse to a duel. Dueling, which originated in sixteenth-century Italy before gaining popularity throughout Europe, generally followed a protocol. The insulted party would throw down his glove before demanding "satisfaction" from the other party. Apparently, this satisfaction could only be obtained by shooting at him.

What happened if a duel ended in a tie? Who won satisfaction?

Actually, duels that ended in a tie were rather commonplace. Not all duels were fought "to the death"; duels could also be fought "to the blood," in which the first man who drew blood from his opponent was the victor. In the case of pistol dueling, "to the blood" meant that each man was allowed only one shot. (Ultimately, the act of the duel itself was enough to save the honor of the participants, and many a duel ended with the two parties simply firing into the air.)

Pistol dueling is what most people think of when they imagine duels, though before the advent of guns, weapons such as swords were used. And even after pistols became fashionable, gentlemen sometimes chose other weapons to defend their honor. One apocryphal tale tells of an aborted duel in the mid-eighteen hundreds between Otto von Bismarck and his nemesis Rudolf Virchow, in which sausages (those wacky Germans!) were chosen as the weapon.

One of the most famous duels that ended in a tie occurred in 1826 between two United States senators, Henry Clay of Mississippi and John Randolph of Virginia. Clay was known as a firebrand, and when he and Randolph disagreed on an issue, Clay demanded satisfaction. The much-ballyhooed duel took place on April 8. Each senator was allowed one shot; naturally, they both missed. It's yet another example of the inability of politicians to do much of anything right.

Duels are no longer an accepted social custom; virtually every country has outlawed them. Still, there's no law against throwing down one's glove and demanding satisfaction.

Q Whatever happened to toga parties?

A In the 1978 movie *Animal House,* John "Bluto" Blutarsky and his fellow Delta House reprobates throw the mother of all toga parties. *Animal House* was a smash hit. Everyone wanted to be like Bluto, and toga parties became a staple of fraternity houses from coast to coast.

The idea was simple: You fashioned a bed sheet, preferably a white one, into a Roman-style toga (think Julius Caesar and company). As the party revved up and the beer began flowing, the guys tried to coax the girls out of their bed sheets and onto the sheets of their beds.

For the most part, college toga parties have gone the way of Roman civilization. Why? Part of the reason may be that kids don't fit into bed sheets like they used to. Around the mid-1990s, astute scientists discovered that Americans were getting fatter. According to the National Association of Children's Hospitals, obesity-related hospital costs for children and young adults more than tripled between 1979 and 1999.

The collective enlargement of the American ass took much of the shine off toga parties. A bed sheet, after all, isn't the optimal way for a self-conscious college student to hide rolls of blubber.

Compounding the issue is the infamous "Freshman Fifteen," a reference to the idea that first-year college students supposedly pack on about fifteen pounds. David A. Levitsky, a professor of nutritional sciences at Cornell University, says the Freshman Fifteen isn't just an urban legend. He conducted a study and concluded: "Significant weight gain during the first semester of college is a real phenomenon, with breakfast and lunch at all-you-can-eat dining facilities accounting for 20 percent of the weight gain."

None of the math works in favor of toga parties. The average twin bed sheet in a dorm room is thirty-nine inches by seventy-five inches; the average eighteen-year-old male who would drunkenly don a toga stands five feet, ten inches. By the second semester of his freshman year, he has slammed down enough beer and Monte Cristo sandwiches to push his waistline past thirty-six inches. That leaves three spare inches of fabric at most to fasten around his bulging gut. Solving this tricky equation would take movie magic—the same kind that enabled *Animal Houses*'s Blutarsky, played by the hefty John Belushi, to fit into his toga.

Enter the "Pimp 'n' Ho" party, today's answer to the toga party. Porky frat boys and sorority girls are much more comfortable—both literally and figuratively—at this type of theme party. Worn-out bed sheets have been swapped for thrift-store leopard robes and fuzzy purple hats. The guys can cover themselves completely and still be part of the theme; the girls can show some skin but have more options for covering unsightly areas than a toga provides.

The "Pimp 'n' Ho" party also fits well into the contemporary musical landscape. What type of musical image does a toga party conjure for today's kids? Some stiff playing a lute. Today's college-age

Americans want to bump and grind, and trying to do that while wearing a bed sheet can create unwanted chafing in the areas down yonder.

The remaining torchbearers for the toga party are guys who want to sleep with the dean's wife. But how often are they going to find and seduce the hot, drunken wife of a college administrator?

Q What did headhunters do with the heads?

A The practice of cutting off your enemy's head and taking it with you dates to at least the Stone Age, about six hundred thousand years ago. Human headhunting was practiced in Africa, South America, New Zealand, Asia, and Indonesia.

Aboriginal Australians and tribes such as the Dayak in Borneo believed that the head contained the victim's spirit or soul. Taking the head, they thought, took the essence of a person's soul as well as his strength. Chinese soldiers during the Qin Dynasty (221–206 BC) carried the heads of conquered enemies into battle to frighten their foes. The heads also served as proof of kills, which enabled soldiers to be paid.

Headhunting wasn't always associated with war. The ancient Celts, for example, incorporated it into fertility rites and other ritualistic practices.

One problem for headhunters was that it doesn't take long for a severed head to begin to decompose. Some headhunters kept only the skull; they cleaned and boiled the head to remove all tissue and brain matter. Others cooked and ate parts of the head, literally consuming the essence of the conquered foe. Still others painstakingly preserved the heads, some of which are with us still.

In New Zealand, Maori headhunters removed the flesh from the skulls of their enemies, then smoked and dried it. This process preserved distinctive tribal tattoos, which meant that the deceased could be identified. Some of these heads were eventually sold to Europeans for private collections or museums, and Maori are today attempting to reclaim the dried heads of their ancestors. In New Guinea, tribes mummified the entire head and sometimes wore it as a mask.

Some of the best-preserved heads come from the Jivaro (or Shuar) tribe of South America. These are shrunken heads, known as *tsantsa*. They are unique among headhunting trophies because of the way the Jivaro preserved them.

After killing and decapitating an enemy, the Jivaro cut and peeled the skin from the skull in one piece, they discarded the skull. They then turned the skin inside out and scraped it to remove the tissue. The skin was then boiled for as long as two hours to shrink it to about one-third its original size. After sewing the eyes closed and skewering the mouth shut, the Jivaro filled the skin with hot rocks, being careful not to burn it, and molded the skin as it cooled so it retained its features. Finally, they removed the rocks, filled the skin with hot sand, and finished the process with a smoking technique. The resulting small, hard, dark mass was recognizable as a human head. Today, the Jivaro sell replicas of *tsantsa* to tourists.

There is evidence that some Allied soldiers took skulls as trophies and souvenirs during World War II, and there are indications of similar practices during the Vietnam War. As recently as 2001, the Borneo Dayaks practiced headhunting during conflicts with another ethnic group, the Madurese. Reports of headhunting still surface occasionally, so if you're visiting a remote locale, you are well advised to keep your head about you.

Q Were the *Mayflower* Pilgrims as straitlaced as we learned in school?

A They tried to be. But you know how it goes: A shoe gets unbuckled, a bonnet comes loose, and suddenly your hormones go into overdrive. The next thing you know, your horn o' plenty hath spilleth forth with wicked abundance.

Our modern-day image of the stern, clean-living, God-fearing residents of Plymouth Colony is largely mythical. It's an illusion that took shape during the nineteenth century, as some overzealous Americans attempted to construct an official, more respectable history of their burgeoning nation.

Historians can't even say for certain how many of the approximately one hundred passengers on the *Mayflower* in 1620 were Puritans and how many were just trying to find better lives away from the grueling poverty that gripped England at the time; it's generally believed that there were more of the latter than the former. And they didn't call themselves "Pilgrims"—they were known to have referred to themselves as "Old Planters" and "Old Comers." Draw your own conclusions from that.

While we don't have many racy details about their private lives, we do know that by 1636, the colonists had a published set of laws that listed capital offenses; among them were sodomy, rape, buggery, and some cases of adultery. So they were certainly obsessed with sex, if not necessarily always having it.

Court records from the colony indicate that sex-related crimes were common transgressions. Fornication, which was defined as having sex outside of marriage, was a frequently committed crime, one that often resulted in a fine. Sometimes, the evidence for a conviction consisted solely of the birth of a child in the early months of a marriage.

The only recorded execution for a sex crime occurred in 1642, when seventeen-year-old Thomas Granger was convicted of buggery. The young man had engaged in unfortunate amorous relationships with sheep, and he paid the ultimate price for it.

Less severe penalties (relatively speaking) often consisted of whippings. (Although it must be said that we can think of certain personality types who might choose a life of crime because of that sort of "punishment.") And like what happened to Hester Prynne in Nathaniel Hawthorne's *The Scarlet Letter,* adulterers were sometimes required to wear the capital letters AD on their clothing.

No, the Pilgrims were not exactly saints. But they certainly took their sins seriously.

Q Why didn't the Three Musketeers fight with muskets?

A Alexandre Dumas, a nineteenth-century French author, wrote hundreds of books, plays, articles, and essays. Much of this prodigious output was due to his "writing factory," in which assistants collaborated, with Dumas's input, to produce the work that bore his name. There's an old advertising adage that says, "A camel is a horse designed by committee"; it's just too bad that bit of wisdom wasn't around in Alex's day—it might have prevented him and his assistants from composing a novel about musketeers without putting any muskets in it.

The Three Musketeers is one of the most famous adventure novels in history. For those of you who lived in a cave during childhood, the historical novel follows the trials and travails of His Majesty's Guards Athos, Porthos, and Aramis, and their young protégé D'Artagnan, as they attempt to save the French crown from the secret machinations of Cardinal Richelieu and a mysterious woman named Milady.

Dumas based his tale on real people and events in French history; in fact, literary historians argue that Dumas paved the way for the historical novel of today. Musketeers—or *mousquetaires*—were sixteenth- and seventeenth-century European soldiers who were armed with the new technological weapon of the age, the musket. France had two elite units of musket-bearing soldiers: the *mousquetaires gris* and *mousquetaires noirs*. These soldiers were equally known for their fighting ability and their panache.

Unfortunately, the musket wasn't a practical weapon. The guns could measure longer than five feet and weigh more than twenty pounds. In fact, most musketeers had to carry a separate device just to keep the musket propped up while firing—hardly the kind of weaponry that lent itself to stylish hand-to-hand battles.

Not surprisingly, muskets fell out of favor with elite soldiers who needed mobility, but the musketeers name stuck. Athos, Porthos, and Aramis, as members of the king's elite guard, wouldn't have had much use for unwieldy guns that required several minutes to reload. Instead, they relied on their swords, charm, and delightfully plumed hats.

Though Dumas gestured toward historical accuracy in his works, he wasn't too concerned about it. In truth, Dumas's extravagant tastes and desire for the limelight made him far too worried about cranking out formulaic, plot-heavy tales to concern himself with little details like consistency, believability, theme, or character development. Which leads us to conclude that, while literary historians may call Dumas one of the fathers of the historical novel, he seems more like the forefather of writing for another medium: television.

Q Why did the Romans sell urine?

A Because there was a demand for it. Why the demand? Because Romans used the stuff by the bucketful to clean and dye clothing. Why urine? Because it worked, it was plentiful, and it was cheap. Why on earth did it work? Because the nitrogenous urea in urine generates ammonia when the urine is left standing around, and this ammonia is a disinfecting and bleaching agent.

Some Romans, like many other people of the time, used urine to wash their teeth, too. But before you go dissing the Romans, realize that for more than fifteen hundred years after the Roman Empire peaked, Europeans were still using urine to clean clothes. And the Romans were not slovenly people, relatively speaking.

They were quite the scientists. For example, it's been argued that after the fall of Rome, battlefield medicine didn't return to Roman levels until World War I, and that's partly a function of hygiene. Besides, lots of people today drink their own urine in the name of alternative medicine.

The Romans made extensive use of public baths—a bit of a turn-off to many of us today, but actually a sign of their culture's advancement. (The Romans were great innovators in matters hydraulic, as evidenced by their clever work with aqueducts and plumbing.) In the first century AD, the emperor Vespasian enacted a "urine tax," and with it coined the proverb *pecunia non olet* ("money does not smell"). But pee does. Imagine the troughs at the more than one hundred public baths where urine vendors would collect their wares, which they sold to the multitude of establishments around Rome and elsewhere that cleaned and bleached and performed a kind of dry-cleaning on woolens. A significant number of Romans were employed in the cleaning industry, experts say.

All in all, we moderns would be astonished to learn how "green" the ancients were. They didn't pump crude oil from the earth and make gasoline of it, and they didn't make plastics of whatever it is we use to make plastics. No, they used what was at hand in re-markable ways. And considering how much urine is quite literally at hand, it's no surprise that they found a way to use it.

Q Whose bright idea was it to electrocute criminals?

A Dr. Alfred Southwick. Southwick was a dentist in Buffalo, New York, but he was no simple tooth-driller. Like many of his contemporaries in the Gilded Age of the 1870s and 1880s, he was a broad-minded man who kept abreast of the remarkable scientific developments of the day—like electricity. Though the phenomenon of electric current had been known of for some time, the technology of electricity was fresh—lightbulbs and other electric inventions had begun to be mass produced, and the infrastructure that brought electricity into the businesses and homes of the well-to-do was appearing in the largest cities.

So Southwick's ears perked up when he heard about a terrible ac-cident involving this strange new technology. A man had walked up to one of Buffalo's recently installed generators and decided to see what all the fuss was about. In spite of the protests of the men who were working on the machinery, he touched something he shouldn't have and, to the shock of the onlookers, died instantly. Southwick pondered the situation with a cold, scientific intelli-gence and wondered if the instant and apparently painless death that high voltage had delivered could be put to good use.

Southwick's interest in electrocution wasn't entirely morbid. Death—or more specifically, execution—was much on people's minds in those days. Popular movements advocated doing away with executions entirely, while more moderate reformers simply wanted a new, more humane method of putting criminals to death. Hangings had fallen out of favor due to the potential for gruesome accidents, often caused by the incompetence of hangmen. While the hangman's goal was to break the criminal's neck instantly, a loose knot could result in an agonizingly slow suffocation; a knot that was too tight had the potential to rip a criminal's head clean off.

To prove the worth of his idea, Southwick began experimenting on dogs (you don't want to know) and discussing the results with other scientists and inventors. He eventually published his work and attracted enough attention to earn himself an appointment on the Gerry Commission, which was created by the New York State Legislature in 1886 and tasked with finding the most humane method of execution.

Although the three-person commission investigated several alternatives, eventually it settled on electrocution—in part because Southwick had won the support of the most influential inventor of the day, Thomas Alva Edison, who had developed the incandescent lightbulb and was trying to build an empire of generators and wires to supply (and profit from) the juice that made his lightbulbs glow. Edison provided influential confirmation that an electric current could produce instant death; the legislature was convinced and a law that made electrocution the state's official method of execution was passed.

On August 6, 1890—after much technical debate (AC or DC? How many volts?) and a few experiments on animals (again, you don't want to know)—William Kemmler, an axe murderer, became the first convicted criminal to be electrocuted. Southwick declared it a success, but the reporters who witnessed it felt otherwise. Kemmler had remained alive after the first jolt, foam was oozing from the mask that had been paced over his face as he struggled to breathe. A reporter fainted. A second jolt of several minutes was applied, and Kemmler's clothes and body caught fire. The stench of burned flesh was terrible.

Despite a public outcry, the state of New York remained committed to the electric method of execution. The technology and technique were improved, and eventually other states began to use electrocution as well. Today, nine states still allow use of the electric chair, though lethal injection is the preferred option.

Q What's the most popular car of all time?

A Selling 2,281 of anything per day, every day for more than four decades, is quite an accomplishment. When the *anything* in question is an automobile, it's truly impressive. But that's what it takes to become the most popular car of all time. Just for fun, let's start in the back and work our way to the front of history's garage of bestsellers:

5. Ford Model T: Approximately 16.5 million sold, 1908–1927. The "Tin Lizzie" put America on wheels. Henry Ford's rugged buggy rolled off the world's first large-scale industrial assembly line and into showrooms, where it sold for as little as three hundred dollars. It changed society by liberating millions to work, shop, and explore farther from home than ever before.

4. Volkswagen Beetle: Approximately 21.5 million sold, 1938–2003. The beloved "Bug" scored big by thinking small. Its air-cooled rear-engine layout and rounded body were very basic and remained largely unchanged from the Beetle's inception as the German "people's car." The Beetle was sidetracked by World War II, but regained its status as an icon and roamed the world into the twenty-first century.

3. Volkswagen Golf: Twenty-four million sold and counting, 1974–present. Named for the Gulf Stream air current, this car was originally known in America as the Rabbit; then as the Golf; and starting in 2006, as the Rabbit again. Now in its fifth design generation, this compact front-wheel-drive hatchback is an economy car that people actually aspire to drive.

2. Ford F-Series pickup truck: Twenty-five million sold and counting, 1948–present. Okay, so technically this is not a car. But these workhorses have served nobly through eleven design generations, first as haulers born to a life of labor and eventually—for better or worse—as suburban status symbols. Trends come and go; the F-Series remains. Some early models are collector classics.

1. Toyota Corolla: Thirty-five million sold and counting, 1966–present. Never an excitement machine but always a jewel in the Japanese giant's lineup, the Corolla is named after the Latin word for "small crown." Through nine design generations—at first, rear-wheel drive and barebones basic; from 1983 on, front-wheel-drive and increasingly cushy—Corolla has never veered from its course as reliable, economical transportation.

It's assembled in fourteen countries, including the United States, South Africa, and India, and its design is modified to suit the driving culture of the region into which it's sold. As we said, an average of about 2,281 Corollas are sold daily. That's a lot of tiny tiaras.

Q What's the difference between a commonwealth and a state?

A Of the fifty states in the United States, four are listed in the Constitution as commonwealths: Kentucky, Massachusetts, Pennsylvania, and Virginia. What's up with that? Well, the word "commonwealth" meant something slightly different back in the time of America's infancy than it does now.

When George Washington and company were trying to make a clean break from Britain, the word was used to describe the ideal for which America was pushing: a government run by and for the people (the common folk) within an independent state. A commonwealth was the exact opposite of a monarchy, which was mostly about lifting up the royalty and not so much about the common good. So when America was still under the rule of England, declaring oneself a commonwealth sent a clear message across the Atlantic: "Hey England, we're going to do our own thing!"

Constitutionally, it meant exactly the same thing as being a state, and once America formally separated from England to become an independent democratic country, the term didn't pack a punch anymore. But those four states were listed as commonwealths in the Constitution, and that is what they continue to be.

The term commonwealth has a different meaning nowadays. There are two modern-day commonwealths associated with the

United States: Puerto Rico and the Northern Mariana Islands. Both have governments that are dependent upon the United States but are also separate from it. Puerto Rico and the Northern Mariana Islands are not represented in Congress, and their citizens do not have to pay federal income tax. Their citizens do, however, pay into Social Security and can receive welfare from the U.S. government. The residents of those islands can't vote for a U.S. president, but they are able to serve in the U.S. armed forces.

As for Kentucky, Massachusetts, Pennsylvania, and Virginia, they're commonwealths in name only. There's absolutely no difference between, say, the commonwealth of Virginia and the state of Indiana. Sorry to burst anyone's bubble.

Q Who exactly is Uncle Sam?

A The image of Uncle Sam—a white-haired man sporting a goatee, wearing a star-spangled top hat, and pointing a finger as he says, "I want *you* for the U.S. Army"—is recognized around the world as a symbol of American freedom and patriotism.

By most accounts, this enduring character can be traced to a real person, one Sam Wilson, who was born in 1766 in Massachusetts. When Wilson grew up, he and his brother Ebenezer were in the business of slaughtering, packing, and shipping meat to American soldiers. The meat was packed in barrels that were stamped with the initials U.S.—for United States. Sam's workers and the soldiers who picked up the barrels had a running joke that the initials stood for "Uncle Sam," as Sam Wilson often was called.

The nickname spread, and people began to associate Uncle Sam with the federal government. On September 15, 1961, the eighty-seventh Congress of the United States officially declared Sam Wilson of Troy, New York, to be "the progenitor of America's national symbol of Uncle Sam."

Was Sam Wilson the real Uncle Sam? Sam the meatpacker didn't have facial hair—cartoonists came up with the goatee—but consider this: He is indeed buried in Troy, New York, at Oakwood Cemetery. There's even a prominent marker on his burial place that reads "Uncle Sam." That's good enough for us.

Q Did George Washington really chop down a cherry tree?

A Just about everyone knows the story of George Washington and the cherry tree: In his youth, he took a hatchet to his dad's cherry tree, and when asked about it, he plucked up the courage to admit to his wrongdoing. It's an inspirational tale about the strong moral fiber of America's first president and about the value of telling the truth, even if it casts you in a bad light. It's a terrific lesson to learn, to be sure. Too bad it probably never happened.

The only mention we have of this event comes from a biography of Washington titled *The Life of George Washington: With Curious Anecdotes, Equally Honorable To Himself, And Exemplary To His Young Countrymen.* Quite a mouthful. It was written in 1809, ten years after Washington's death, by a bookseller named M. L. Weems, better known as Parson Weems. The book contained many pieces of factual information, but several legends were also featured, including the story of the cherry tree. By this point, it's impossible to gather any sort of physical evidence about whether the cutting actually occurred, but given that Weems's book is the lone printed reference to it, the story is quite likely a fabrication. Weems claimed that he heard the story from a "distant relative close to the family"—but no Washington family members had ever heard of the tale.

Still, the lesson is a good one: Honesty is always the best policy. And more than just a simple morality lesson, the tale of Washington and the cherry tree served (and continues to serve) an important role in the creation of a national identity. A country needs its heroes, and as shown by such works as *The Odyssey*, the stories that create these heroes need not be dry, factual accounts. It's likely that Weems recognized this and set out to become the next Homer by elevating Washington to a near-mythical status. Whether this was Weems's intention, it worked. The story about the cherry tree is still being told, and Washington is viewed as a paragon of morality, humility, and responsibility.

Q Why did ancient Egyptians shave their eyebrows?

A Shaving away all bodily hair, including eyebrows, was part of an elaborate daily purification ritual that was practiced by Pharaoh and his priests.

The ancient Egyptians believed that everything in their lives—health, good crops, victory, prosperity—depended on keeping their gods happy, so one of Pharaoh's duties was to enter a shrine and approach a special statue of a god three times a day, every day. Each time he visited the shrine, Pharaoh washed the statue, anointed it with oil, and dressed it in fresh linen.

Because Pharaoh was a busy guy, high-ranking priests often performed this duty for him. But whether it was Pharaoh or a priest doing it, the person had to bathe himself and shave his eyebrows beforehand.

Shaving the eyebrows was also a sign of mourning, even among commoners. The Greek historian Herodotus, who traveled and wrote in the fifth century BC, said that everyone in an ancient Egyptian household would shave his or her eyebrows following the natural death of a pet cat. For dogs, he reported, the household members would shave their heads and all of their body hair as well.

Herodotus was known to repeat some wild stories in his books—for instance, he reported that serpents with bat-like wings flew from Arabia into Egypt and were killed in large numbers by ibises. Herodotus claimed he actually saw heaps of these serpent skeletons. So you might want to take his eyebrow-shaving claim with a grain of salt...and a pinch of catnip.

Q What was the first major credit card?

A According to *The Flintstones*, credit cards have been around since the days when humans coexisted with dinosaurs.

The cards were carved from stone, and shoppers paid for their dinosaur-derived luxury items by uttering a guttural, "Charge it!"

In reality, the story goes back only as far as 1949. Frank McNamara (who was head of a credit corporation) and two friends had finished dining at a New York City restaurant, and Frank reached into his pocket to pay for the meal. All he found was lint—he had forgotten his wallet. To avoid washing dishes, McNamara opted for a slightly less embarrassing solution: calling his wife and asking her to bring money.

This brush with empty pockets gave Frank an idea: What if instead of stores each issuing their own lines of credit, thus requiring people to tote around dozens of cards, there was one card that could be used in various places? Since this would require a middleman between customers and businesses, Frank figured he might as well snag the position for himself. And, thus, the Diner's Club card was born.

In 1950, Diner's Club distributed two hundred cards, mainly to McNamara's friends and associates, most of whom where salespeople. Since they had to entertain clients with meals, it was a perfect scenario—they could go to any of the participating restaurants and simply charge their food and drinks.

The first card was not made of plastic—it was paper, with a list of the participating restaurants on the back. Initially, only fourteen restaurants were included, but the idea soon caught on. By the end of 1950, there were twenty thousand card members and one thousand participating restaurants.

After McNamara sold his share of the company in 1952, the Diner's Club concept continued to grow. The card went national and worldwide, eventually facing competition from American Express, Visa, MasterCard, and others. In early 1981, Citibank bought Diner's Club; in April 2008, Discover Financial Services bought Diners Club International from Citibank for $165 million. Not bad for a guy who couldn't afford to pay for dinner.

Chapter Ten

SPORTS

Q Whatever happened to Ted Williams's head?

A Where is Ted's head, anyway? It's in a barrel in Scottsdale, Arizona. To understand why the question and its absurd-sounding answer are significant, it helps to know a little about Theodore Samuel Williams.

Ted Williams was one of the greatest baseball players ever. He is to the Boston Red Sox what Babe Ruth is to the New York Yankees. Among the most feared hitters of all time, Williams is the last major league player to achieve a batting average of .400, hitting .406 in 1941. He's among a handful of players with more than 500 career home runs and was elected to the National Baseball

Hall of Fame in 1966. His incredible baseball career was interrupted twice because he was a fighter pilot—yes, a fighter pilot—in World War II and the Korean War. Williams was a controversial figure—a loner who had a contentious relationship with the media. Williams was also an avid outdoorsman and, after his playing days ended in 1960, was a well-known corporate spokesman for Sears.

Anyhow, Ted's head is currently floating with several other severed heads in a barrel of liquid nitrogen at a "cryonics" facility in Scottsdale. His body is in another barrel, with some other optimistic cadavers.

This has been the case since "Teddy Ballgame" departed this life in 2002. It's the result of a pact that was apparently made between Williams and two of his three adult children to have their bodies cryogenically preserved. His eldest daughter challenged the validity of the pact.

Cryopreservation is the business of deep-freezing human remains shortly after death. The theory—based on various scientific principles—is that if the essential cell structure of a body is preserved, the body can be revived in the future, once the necessary technology has been developed.

Adding to the macabre specter of the "Splendid Splinter" decapitated and bobbing about in a sealed container are reports about the Arizona facility itself. A friend of Williams talked his way in and later told the media about what he regarded as unacceptable conditions, including the indignity of Ted sharing a cylinder with a bunch of average Joes. Other reports allege that some of the 182 samples of Williams's DNA that were preserved by the lab are missing.

The body of Williams's only son, John-Henry, followed Ted to the Scottsdale facility after his own death in 2004. Judging from accounts, the elder Williams was not an easy man to have as a father, and John-Henry didn't behave like a prince of a son. Here's hoping that medical science someday succeeds in reanimating those who forked over more than $100,000 to become popsicles—Ted's bill reportedly was $136,000—and that the Williams family gets along better the next time around.

Q Why isn't a boxing ring round?

A Boxing has been around for ages because, when you get down to it, humans like to pummel each other. The ancient Greeks were the ones who decided to make it into a legitimate sport: Boxing was introduced as an Olympic event in 688 BC. The competitors wrapped pieces of soft leather around their hands and proceeded to fight.

The Romans took it a little further, adding bits of metal to the leather. No wonder those guys ruled most of the known world for so long!

Fast forward to England in the eighteenth century. Boxing was popular—and it was violent. The fighters battled each other inside a ring of rope that was lined with—and sometimes held up by—spectators. That's right, a *ring*. These spectators couldn't be counted on to be sober and often raucously crowded the boxers—the rope ring would get smaller and smaller until the onlookers were practically on top of the fighters. Often the spectators would have a go at it with the boxers themselves.

Understandably, the fighters got a bit testy about the situation. Jack Broughton, a heavyweight champion, came up with a set of rules to protect his fellow boxers in 1743. His plan included a chalked-off square inside which the boxers would fight. Event organizers attached rope to stakes that were pounded into the ground, which prevented the fighting area from changing sizes and from being invaded. Why a square? Because it was easy to make.

Broughton's rules were eventually revised to formalize the square shape. By 1853, the rules stated that matches had to take place in a twenty-four-foot square "ring" that was enclosed by ropes. That, good reader, is the origin of what boxing aficionados call "the squared circle."

Q In bowling, why are three strikes in a row called a Turkey?

A We love bowling. Love the mustaches, the tinted glasses, the fingerless gloves. We love that air-vent thingy on the ball rack, and we love the swirling balls that are inscribed with names like Lefty and Dale. We love the satin shirts and multi-colored shoes (okay, maybe not the shoes so much). But what we love most are the terms. The Dutch 200, the Brooklyn strike, the Cincinnati, the Jersey, the Greek Church, and especially the Turkey. We have no idea what any of these terms mean, but we love them all the same.

Believe it or not, bowling wasn't always the sexy, hip sport played by highly trained athletes that it is today. Some historians trace bowling's roots back to 3200 BC, while others place its origin in

Europe in the third century AD. Regardless, some form of bowling has been popular for centuries. For much of this history, however, bowling didn't have a particularly sterling reputation. Quite the opposite: Legend holds that King Edward III banned bowling after his good-for-nothing soldiers kept skipping archery practice to roll. And well into the nineteenth century, American towns were passing laws that forbid bowling, largely because of the gambling that went along with it.

Despite these attempts at suppression—or perhaps because of them—bowling increased in popularity. In 1895, the American Bowling Congress (now known as the United States Bowling Congress) was formed, and local and regional bowling clubs began proliferating. It was around this time that the term "Turkey," which signifies three strikes in a row, came into being.

In an attempt to cash in on the burgeoning popularity of the newly sanctioned sport, as well as draw customers, many bowling alley proprietors offered a free live turkey to bowlers who successfully rolled three strikes in a row during Thanksgiving or Christmas week. Sadly, turkeys are no longer awarded at bowling alleys, although the tradition of shouting "Turkey" when somebody manages three strikes in a row continues.

So the next time you cry "fowl" at the bowling alley, you can take pride in knowing that you're continuing a time-honored tradition. Now if we could just figure out who decided two-toned bowling shoes were a good idea, we'd really be on to something.

Q Did Abner Doubleday really invent baseball?

A Along with the Easter Bunny and Santa Claus, the story of Abner Doubleday inventing baseball in 1839 in Cooperstown, New York, is a fabrication.

Doubleday was a West Point cadet and a Civil War veteran, as well as an unwitting party to the myth that he invented baseball. Ol' Abner didn't go around patting himself on the back for graduating from West Point, commanding troops, or inventing America's pastime. Thousands of pieces of correspondence were in Doubleday's possession at the time of his death in 1893, and not one mentioned baseball.

It was the National Baseball Hall of Fame and Museum in—you guessed it—Cooperstown that wanted to draw a connection between itself and the invention of baseball (purportedly in a local cow pasture). The Hall of Fame interviewed just one witness, Abner Graves, before citing Doubleday as the inventor of baseball. While it was bad enough to take a single person's testimony as uncontestable evidence, Graves made the Hall's case look worse in 1924, when he shot his wife and was declared criminally insane.

In reality, baseball evolved from many different bat-and-ball games, such as the English games of cricket and rounders, as well as an American game, town ball. It's not as if someone sat down and wrote the rules for baseball from scratch, as James Naismith did for basketball.

However, a man named Alexander Cartwright can be credited with at least drawing up the basic parameters of baseball and determining the measurements of the diamond. Cartwright played town ball for the New York Knickerbockers, and in 1845, he and some of his teammates created a game they called baseball, which was designed to be a more intricate version of town ball.

Among Cartwright's guidelines were three strikes per out, three outs per inning, nine players per team, ninety feet between bases, and the concept of fair and foul territory. One major difference between baseball and town ball was that in Cartwright's baseball, a runner couldn't be "soaked"—declared out on the basepath after being hit by a fielder's thrown ball. Cartwright's Knickerbockers and the New York Nine played the first game using the new rules on June 19, 1846; the Nine trounced the Knickerbockers, 23 to 1.

How did baseball spread across the country and become the national pastime? Cartwright went west in search of gold in 1849, and he introduced baseball to people along the way. He later settled in Hawaii and set up some of the first baseball leagues. The Hall of Fame may not properly credit Cartwright, but the U.S. Congress did in 1953 by formally recognizing him as the inventor of baseball.

Q How do bookies set odds on sporting events?

A To answer this question, we need to learn a little about the sports book biz. Consider this gambling primer: Bookies take a small percentage of every bet that comes in; this is known as the vig. The ideal situation for any bookie is to have an equal amount of money riding on both sides of a bet; this way, no matter what happens in the game, the bookie will make money. The bookie will pay out money to those who bet on the winner, take in money from those who bet on the loser, and come out ahead because of the vig.

If everyone bets on one team and that team wins, the bookie will lose a lot of money. Sports odds are designed to keep an even number of bettors on each side of the bet.

Major sports books in Las Vegas and Europe employ experienced oddsmakers to set the point spread, odds, or money line on a game. Oddsmakers must know a lot about sports and a lot about gamblers: They examine every detail of an upcoming game—including public perceptions about it—to determine which team has the better chance of winning. Several days or weeks prior to the game, the oddsmakers meet, compare information, and reach a consensus on the odds.

Here's a simple example: Team A is thought to be much better than Team B in an upcoming game. If both sides of the bet paid off the same amount of money, almost everyone would bet on Team A. The oddsmakers try to determine what odds will even out the betting. Giving Team B five-to-one odds means anyone who bets on Team B will make five times his bet if Team B wins. Team B may not have much of a chance of winning, but the increased reward makes the risk worthwhile to gamblers.

Or, depending on the sport and the country, the oddsmakers might set a money line, which is usually expressed as a "plus" or "minus" dollar amount. This is effectively the same thing as setting odds—the money line simply reflects the payoff that a bettor can expect from a winning bet.

Another way to balance the betting market is with a point spread. In this case, winning bets always pay off at one-to-one, or even odds, usually with a 10 percent vig on top, which means you would have to bet eleven dollars to win ten dollars. The point spread handicaps the game in favor of one team. In, say, football, Team A might get a spread of minus-seven. This means gamblers aren't just betting on whether Team A will win, but on whether it will do so by more than seven points.

Odds can change leading up to an event. This might indicate something significant happened, such as an injury to a key player, or it might mean that bookies are adjusting the odds because too many bets were coming in on one side. Adjusting the odds reflects their attempt to balance the betting and minimize their potential loss. Remember, a bookie isn't in this for fun and games—he's in it to make profits. And at the end of the day, he's the one who almost always wins.

Q Why do golfers yell "Fore!" when they hit an errant shot?

A No one has a definite answer. There are only theories—some logical, some far-fetched enough to include warnings between artillery gunners and golfers outside a Scottish fort in the late sixteenth century. Some version of the shout goes back more than a century; it turns up as common etiquette in Robert Forgan's 1881 version of *The Golfer's Handbook*. Before that, who knows?

The United States Golf Association (USGA) agrees that "fore" is Scottish in origin and suggests it's a version of a warning that meant "look out ahead" in military circles. The USGA's conclusion is that the old military term—which was used by artillery men to troops in forward positions—simply got adopted by golfers around the eighteenth century. That's one possibility.

Then there is the issue of the "forecaddie," a person who is retained to go ahead of players to mark the lies of balls in play. Here's that theory, according to the British Golf Museum: "It may be that, over time, the word forecaddie was shortened when yelled as warning to this person and the word has remained in use since."

The simplest explanation might be the one offered up by Brent Kelley in *Your Guide to Golf*. "Fore is another word for 'ahead' (think of a ship's fore and aft)," Kelley wrote. "Yelling 'fore' is simply a shorter way to yell 'watch out ahead.'"

Neil JB Laird did a thorough background search of the word "fore" in the book *Scottish Golf History,* which was published in 2003. Laird acknowledges that "...no certain etymology for the golf word 'Fore!' has been agreed." However, he proposes three possibilities:

First, that it was indeed shouted as a warning to forecaddies, who were supposed to stand as close as possible to where a shot would land. Laird points out that forecaddies originally were employed because golf balls were expensive and players didn't want to lose them.

Second, that the exclamation comes from military battles in the musket era, when various ranks would fire over the heads of their comrades. There is speculation that the word "fore" was used to warn soldiers in front to keep their heads down.

Third, that gunners might have been giving fair warning to nearby golfers. The excavation of a place called Ramsay's Fort, a sixteenth-century fortification outside Leith, Scotland, shows the fort overlooked Leith Links, a golf course that still exists today. Laird suggests that because the people of Leith were quite well connected politically, gunners at the fort might have yelled out to them before they began firing practice—and that eventually the golfers simply picked up the term themselves.

Q In hockey, why is scoring three goals called a hat trick?

A The sports world is full of weird, wonderful jargon. Third base in baseball is called "the hot corner." In football, a deep pass thrown up for grabs is known as a "Hail Mary." In hockey, scoring three goals is labeled a "hat trick." The first term makes sense, the second one kind of makes sense, and the third one is completely baffling. Throughout most of hockey's history, players didn't wear helmets, let alone hats. What gives?

Etymologists agree that the term "hat trick" originated in cricket, a British game that few Americans care about or understand. Evidently, back in the mid-1850s, when a cricket "bowler" captured three consecutive "wickets," he earned a free hat. Though we have no idea what that means, it still raises the question: How did the term "hat trick" infiltrate the lexicon of hockey, another game that few Americans care about or understand?

As legend has it, hockey's use of "hat trick" originated in the early 1940s with a Toronto haberdasher (someone who sells hats) named

Sammy Taft. The story goes that a Chicago Blackhawks forward named Alex Kaleta visited Taft's shop one day in search of a new fedora, only to find that Taft's hats were too pricey for his meager professional athlete's salary (my, how times have changed).

Taft, feeling generous, offered to give Kaleta the hat for free if he could score three goals in that evening's game against the Toronto Maple Leafs. Kaleta did, and the hat was his. Taft, sensing a potential marketing boon, made a standing offer to any player who could score three goals in a Maple Leafs home game. Sometimes he even threw the prize hat onto the ice after the third goal. The hat-tossing became a fad, and soon other fans—apparently far wealthier than poor Kaleta—were tossing their hats onto the ice.

For many hockey fans, any excuse to throw something onto the ice is cause for celebration. Besides hats, octopuses have been tossed onto the rink by fans in Detroit, and in Florida the lovely tradition of throwing rats onto the ice began after a Panthers player scored two goals in a game after killing a rat in the locker room. It's a far cry from the heart-warming tradition started by Sammy Taft. Then again, the whole concept of hockey in Florida is pretty weird in itself.

Q Why are ineligible college athletes called redshirts?

A Ask *Star Trek* fans what a "redshirt" is, and they'll tell you that it's a term that's used to describe a stock character who is introduced into a storyline, only to be killed by the end of the episode. Ask Italians what a "redshirt" is, and they'll point to a portrait of Giuseppe Garibaldi as they hum a few bars of Italy's national anthem. Ask college football fans what a "redshirt" is, and they'll stare at you blankly for a few minutes before asking you to pass the chips.

This is not so much a reflection of the IQ of the average football fan as it is of the general confusion surrounding the term "redshirt." Part of the problem is this: Although the term is bandied about quite often in discussions of college sports, "redshirt" isn't an official term of the governing body of college athletics, the National Collegiate Athletic Association (NCAA). Furthermore, try as you might, you won't find any college athletes sitting on the sidelines actually wearing red shirts—unless red is the color of their uniform, of course.

Much of the confusion is rooted in the NCAA's rules of eligibility for college athletes. Essentially, all college athletes are given, upon initial enrollment, five years to complete four years of competition. Because of this rule, some college athletes skip a season of play in order to extend their eligibility. In order to earn a fifth year of eligibility, the player must not participate in any sanctioned competition during the skipped season. Not one play in a football game, not one pitch in a baseball game—any participation whatsoever uses up one year of eligibility. There are hundreds of detailed rules that further define eligibility; in fact, many college athletic departments have entire divisions devoted to merely interpreting and applying the rules for their own players.

College athletes might choose to sit out a season for a number of reasons, including injury, academic issues, or because the player isn't physically and/or mentally ready to play at the college level. These athletes are allowed to practice with the team, essentially making the skipped season an extended training session. When this practice first started in college sports, these athletes would wear red shirts during practice to differentiate them from eligible players—hence the term "redshirts." The word entered the lexicon in September 1950, according to the *Oxford English Dictionary,* when it was used in a Birmingham, Alabama, newspaper article.

Nowadays, red-shirting is a common practice. College sports are multibillion-dollar industry, and the players are auditioning for multimillion-dollar jobs in the professional ranks. So the next time you're watching the big game at a buddy's house and the announcer refers to a player as a redshirt freshman, you can enlighten your friends about the term and its origin. Just make sure to pass the chips first.

Q Why do baseball managers and coaches wear uniforms instead of street clothes?

A Coaches in basketball, football, hockey, and soccer are content to wear street clothes, and some, such as Pat Riley in the NBA, have even garnered extra respect for their sartorial strategies. Yet managers and coaches in baseball dress just like the players. What gives?

More than any other sport, baseball clings to its traditions—not unlike the way a stretchy polyester uniform clings to the expanding midsection of an aging manager. Despite such modern phenomena as free agency, domed stadiums, and sausage races, today's baseball culture still has roots in the game's distant past.

In the nineteenth century, ball clubs really were clubs—fraternities that played baseball by day and gathered at night for formal parties, where players ate, drank, socialized, and sang special club songs. The uniforms they wore were almost sacred articles that distinguished the players not only from those of rival ball clubs but also—and perhaps more importantly—from spectators and the rest of society at large.

In those early days, the captain of the team held the responsibilities of a modern-day manager: creating lineups, making key tactical decisions, and kicking dirt on the shoes of an unsympathetic umpire. As the game evolved and the century turned, the more successful captains found work as managers after their playing days were over. But since they were unwilling to surrender their membership in the fraternity of baseball, they continued to wear their uniforms.

There were exceptions—most famously, Connie Mack, who managed the Philadelphia Athletics for a preposterously long time, from 1901 to 1950. A former major-league player, Mack nevertheless wore a suit and tie when he managed the A's. Perhaps not coincidentally, Mack also owned the franchise, so his ties to the fraternity were likely not as strong as those of most managers.

There are some practical considerations. Many baseball coaches spend time on the field before the game instructing players, leading them in warm-ups, and hitting ground balls to infielders—all of which would be difficult to accomplish in a suit and tie. What's more, the official rules of Major League Baseball stipulate that first- and third-base coaches should be in uniform. There's no mention of the manager, though; in fact, rule 3.15 states, in part, "No person shall be allowed on the playing field during a game except players and coaches in uniform, managers, [and] news photographers..." The rule book seems to be saying, indirectly, that the manager doesn't need to be in uniform.

But an incident in 2007, during which a representative from the baseball commissioner's office harassed Boston Red Sox manager Terry Francona during a game for not complying with the league's dress code (Francona sometimes preferred to wear a Red Sox pull-over instead of the regulation uniform top), suggests that today's baseball uniform remains every bit as sacred as the sausage race.

Chapter Eleven

EARTH AND SPACE

Q Why are you colder on a mountain, even though you're closer to the sun?

A This question assumes you might think that the only factor influencing temperature is proximity to that fireball in the sky. In other words, this question assumes you might be an idiot. It's much more complicated than proximity.

It has to be, or else the lowest nighttime temperatures on Mercury, which is two-and-a-half times closer to the sun than Earth is, wouldn't be –297 degrees

Fahrenheit. And the moon, which is sometimes 240,000 miles closer to the sun than Earth is, wouldn't get as cold as –280 degrees Fahrenheit.

The reason it's colder on a mountaintop is because at that altitude, the atmosphere is different. Specifically, the air pressure is lower. The pressure at the top of Mount Everest, which is five-and-a-half miles above sea level, is less than a third of what it is at sea level.

During July—the warmest month on Everest—the average temperature hovers around –2 degrees Fahrenheit. It doesn't get above freezing up there, ever.

In simplest terms, when air is put under more pressure, it gets warmer. When the pressure lessens, it gets colder. That's why a bicycle pump warms up when you pump up a tire—in addition to the friction that's caused by the piston inside, the pump creates air pressure. It's also why an aerosol can gets downright cold if you spray it too long—air pressure escapes from the can.

When you think about all this, you realize how many scientific factors combine to make Earth hospitable for life. The moon has no atmosphere whatsoever; Mercury has a minute amount of it. The precise combination of gases that make up our atmosphere accounts for the air we breathe, the way the sun warms it, the color of the sky, and myriad other factors that explain life as we know it.

In fact, the cold temperatures at the top of a mountain are pretty minor when it comes to the miraculous—but scientifically logical—realities that are related to atmosphere.

Q Why are planets round?

A We all know about gravity. When something is really heavy (the size of a planet, for example), it pulls other objects toward it. That's why we don't float off Earth—it's holding us down. Technically, we're also pulling Earth toward us, but because we're so small and Earth is so large, we don't really affect it much.

Now, everything on a planet is being pulled toward its heavy center because of the planet's gravity, and everything is drawn as close to the center as possible. The only way for everything on the surface to be equally close to the center is for the planet to be round; each point on the surface of a sphere is the same distance from its center.

If a planet were, say, a cube, its corners would be farther from the center than everything else. Because of gravity, these corners would collapse inward to get closer to the center. After this collapse and the planet's subsequent reformation, it would end up being a good old sphere.

But like its human inhabitants, Earth is not perfect. It bulges slightly at its middle (the equator) because it is spinning. Its shape, then, is somewhat wonky; Earth's equator is more than a dozen miles farther from the planet's center than are the North and South poles. The technical term for Earth's shape is "oblate spheroid." Most planets are oblate spheroids. Saturn is the most noticeably wonky—its equator is 10 percent fatter than its polar diameter. Throw that at your friends the next time there's a lull in the conversation, and watch them bow to your genius.

Q Why are most plants green?

A Maybe they're envious of our ability to walk over to the sink and get a drink of water.

While that theory is certainly compelling, plants aren't green with envy. The green comes from a pigment called chlorophyll. Pigments are substances that absorb certain wavelengths of light and reflect others. In other words, pigments determine color—you see the wavelength of light that the pigment reflects. A plant is green because the chlorophyll in it is really good at absorbing red and blue light but lousy at absorbing green light.

You find a heaping helping of chlorophyll in plants because chlorophyll's job is to absorb sunlight for use in photosynthesis, which is the process of converting sunlight and carbon dioxide into food (carbohydrates) that plants need to survive. So, since a plant wouldn't get too far without delicious carbs, just about every plant is partially green. This isn't true across the board, though. Some plants use different pigments for photosynthesis, and there are a few hundred parasitic plant species that don't need chlorophyll because they mooch carbohydrates that are produced by other plants. But for the most part, land plants depend on chlorophyll to maintain their active plant lifestyle. And by extension, so do we, since animal life depends on plants to survive.

But why reflect green and absorb red and blue rather than the other way around? The short answer is that the red and the blue light are the good stuff. The sun emits more red photons than any other color, and blue photons carry more energy than other colors. Sunlight is abundant enough that it wouldn't be efficient to absorb all light, so plants evolved to absorb the areas of the light spectrum that offer the best bang for the buck. And it's a good thing, too: If plants needed to absorb the full spectrum of sunlight to get by, they would all be black. And the outdoors would have a decidedly gloomy tint.

Q Why are some bodies of water salty and others are not?

A Actually, all bodies of water contain salt. When the salt concentration is high, as in the oceans, it's obvious to the human tongue. In so-called freshwater lakes and rivers, the concentration is much lower—so low that the tongue can't detect it—but the salt is still there.

When oceanographers discuss the salt content (or salinity) of water, they refer to the concentration in terms of parts per thousand. For instance, the saltiest waters in the world—the Red Sea and the Persian Gulf—contain forty pounds of salt for every thousand pounds of water. The major oceans have thirty-five parts per thousand.

In contrast, the Great Lakes—the largest freshwater bodies in the world—contain less than an ounce of salt per thousand pounds of water. Your taste buds would have to be mighty sensitive to be able to pick out a salty taste in these waters.

Bodies of water are saltier in regions with higher temperatures; the higher the mercury rises, the more water is evaporated. When water evaporates, salt is left behind. The evaporated water forms clouds that hover high over land and eventually produce rain. The rainwater drains into a river system and picks up salty minerals from the riverbed. When the river rejoins the ocean, it adds more salt to the already salty waters.

This process is what makes Utah's Great Salt Lake so salty. Numerous rivers and streams empty into the lake, carrying with them the same minerals that contribute to an ocean's salinity. Since the Great Salt Lake has no outlet, the minerals that enter have nowhere to go. As a result, some sections of the lake have salinity levels that are eight times higher than those of the saltiest oceans. Salinity in the Great Salt Lake ranges from one hundred and fifty to one hundred and sixty parts per thousand.

You can infer, then, that the saltwater bodies with the lowest salinity would be located in cold regions: the Arctic Ocean, the seas around Antarctica, and the Baltic Sea. The last of these ranges in salinity from five to fifteen parts per thousand. These bodies of water are constantly being diluted by melting ice and continued precipitation, and they evaporate at much slower rates than hotter oceans and seas; they're always getting more water, but rarely more salt.

Drinking saltwater can throw off your body's natural sodium levels, resulting in dehydration. Tap water generally does not have high enough salinity to pose a threat to the average, healthy adult. But the EPA and the American Heart Association have recommended that those who have been instructed to maintain a strict no-salt diet should stay away from water with higher salinity than twenty parts per million. Bottled water has been suggested as a safe alternative, but be sure to check the sodium content on the nutritional label. Even bottled water, it seems, isn't always "fresh."

Q Why is Pluto not a planet anymore?

A Poor Pluto. It was welcomed into the exclusive club of planets in 1930 after being discovered by American astronomer Clyde Tombaugh, but then was unceremoniously booted out on August 24, 2006, by the International Astronomical Union (AIU). Because Pluto's orbit around the sun takes approximately 247.9 Earth years, it didn't even get to celebrate its first anniversary of being a planet.

Pluto didn't change. What did?

The word and original definition of "planet" are derived from the Greek *asteres planetai,* which means "wandering stars." Planets are known as wanderers because they appear to move against the relatively fixed background of the stars, which are much more distant. Five planets (Mercury, Venus, Mars, Jupiter, and Saturn) are visible to the naked eye from Earth and were known to people in ancient times.

Three other planets would not have been discovered without modern advancements. Uranus was discovered by William Herschel in 1781, using a telescope; Johanne Galle discovered Neptune in 1846, using sophisticated mathematical predictions; and Pluto was discovered when the astronomer Tombaugh laboriously flipped through photographic plates of regions of the sky captured at different dates that showed the special wandering that denotes a planet.

Continued improvements in telescopes and mathematical modeling, among other advancements, have helped astronomers find all sorts of things in a solar system that previously seemed somewhat vacant. Classifying all of these objects—especially with respect to what is a planet and what's not—has proven to be tricky. On August 24, 2006, the IAU established a cut-and-dried definition of a planet. To be a planet, an object must orbit the sun, have enough mass so that it is nearly round, and dominate the area around its orbit.

This turn of events was bad news for Pluto because it doesn't meet the third part of the definition—it doesn't dominate its "neighborhood." For one thing, planets are supposed to be much larger than their moons, and Pluto's moon, Charon, is about half its size. Second, a planet is supposed to clear the neighborhood around its orbit—meaning it should, in the words of *National Geographic News,* "sweep up asteroids, comets, and other debris"—and Pluto isn't particularly effective at doing that.

The IAU didn't completely diss Pluto. It now is classified as a dwarf planet, meaning that it orbits the sun, is round, and isn't a satellite of any other object, despite not clearing its orbit. There are dozens of known dwarf planets, and scientists expect the number to grow rapidly because so many objects fit the criteria.

NASA also has given Pluto its due (though it did so before it was declassified as a planet). On January 19, 2006, NASA launched an unmanned probe called New Horizons that is bound for Pluto. After traveling three billion miles, the probe is expected to enter the Pluto system in the summer of 2015. It carries some of the ashes of Tombaugh, who no doubt would have been horrified to learn that his grand discovery has been reduced to a dwarf.

Q What's a green flash?

A The logical answer would be a comic book superhero—a cross between the Green Lantern and the Flash. But that isn't it. A green flash comes from nature, not the mind of a geeky writer. It's a phenomenon that occurs at sunset or sunrise, during which part of the sun seems to change in color to green or emerald. The term "flash" is used to describe the change because it is visible for only a second or two.

Green flashes are so rarely seen that they have reached an almost mythological status. Some say they don't really exist—that they're just a mirage; others insist they do exist, but only in remote parts of the world. There's a mountain of misinformation about green flashes, dating back at least to the science fiction pioneer Jules Verne. In his 1882 novel *Le Rayon-Vert,* Verne wrote that a person who was "fortunate enough once to behold [a green flash] is enabled to see closely into his own heart and to read the thoughts of others." A green flash is remarkable, yes … but not that remarkable.

A green flash is the result of three optical phenomena: refraction near the horizon, scattering, and absorption. Refraction is the bending of a light wave as it travels through another medium. Scattering occurs when a light wave travels through particles whose diameter is no more than one-tenth the length of the light wave. Absorption occurs when a light wave reaches a material whose electrons are vibrating at the same frequency as one or more of the colors of light.

At sunset, the image of the sun that you can see is slightly above the actual position of the sun. This is caused by refraction, which separates the solar light into wavelengths, or colors. Although the atmosphere barely absorbs yellow light, even a little bit of absorption can make a big difference when the sun is near the horizon. The blue light is scattered away. So, what you have is the ray of red light "setting" at a very particular moment and no longer reaching your eye, the ray of yellow light being absorbed and no longer reaching your eye, and the ray of blue light being scattered about the atmosphere and no longer reaching your eye. The result is a momentary ray of green light—a green flash.

If you want to see a green flash, we have some tips. First and foremost, be patient and accept that you may never see one. However, if you know when and from where to look, and under what conditions, you might become one of the lucky observers of a green flash.

Find a place from which you have an unobstructed view of the horizon. Mountains are the best vantage point. Beaches are second-best because you can use the ocean line as your guide. Other high places, such as an in-flight airplane or a tall building, will also do. You need to be in an area where the sky is cloudless and the air is clean; if the air is dusty, smoggy, or hazy, the green wavelengths won't be transmitted. You'll also want to have binoculars, because a green flash is very small.

Finally, be smart. Remember when your mom would tell you not to stare at the sun? Smart lady. At sunset, don't look at the sun until it is nearly down; at sunrise, start looking just as the sun seems ready to peek over the horizon. Staring at that big ball of fire at the wrong time can permanently bleach the red-sensitive photopigment in your eyes, forever distorting your color perception. Happy hunting.

Q Why aren't there southern lights?

A There are. The southern lights are called the "aurora australis," and according to those who've seen them (including famed explorer Captain James Cook, who named the lights in 1773), they are just as bright and alluring as the aurora borealis in the north. We don't hear about them because the viewing area—around the geomagnetic South Pole—is mostly unpopulated.

Northern or southern, the lights are the result of solar storms that emit high-energy particles. These particles travel from the sun as a solar wind until they encounter and interact with the earth's magnetic field. They then energize oxygen atoms in the upper atmosphere, causing light emissions that can appear to us as an arc, a curtain, or a green glow. If these oxygen atoms get really excited, they turn red.

There are other atoms in the ionosphere, and they produce different colors when they're titillated by those solar winds. Neutral nitrogen will produce pink lights, and nitrogen radicals glow blue and violet.

Usually, the lights are visible only in latitudes between ninety degrees (at the poles) and thirty degrees. In the north, that large swath includes most of Europe, Asia (excluding India, except for its northernmost tip, and southern countries such as Myanmar, Thailand, and Cambodia), the United States, and Canada. In the south, though, only the southernmost tips of Australia and Africa and the countries of Chile, Argentina, and Uruguay in South America are within that zone.

So in reality the question is this: If a light shines in the south and there is no one there to see it, does it still dazzle?

Q Was a day always twenty-four hours long?

A From almost the first moment humans decided that a day needed more segmentation than the obvious day and night, twenty-four has been the number of choice.

The practice began thirty-five hundred years ago, with the invention of the Egyptian sundial. Before then, humans had little interest in specifying the time of day. It was enough to differentiate between morning and evening by using an obelisk—a four-sided monument that cast a westward shadow in the pre-noon hours and an eastward shadow as evening approached.

The sundial divided a day into twelve hours of light and twelve hours of darkness—though, of course, it was capable of displaying the time only during sunlight hours. The Egyptians marked an hour of twilight at sunrise, an hour of twilight at sunset, and ten hours in between. Nighttime hours were approximated by the use of decan stars (stars that rise in the hours before dawn). Twelve decan stars rise in the Egyptian sky during the summer months. Historians believe that these stars might be the reason the earliest timekeepers chose to base their sundials on the number twelve.

The hour did not have a set length until the second century BC— thirteen hundred years later. Until then, the length of the hour changed as the seasons changed. During winter months, nighttime hours were longer; during summer months, daytime hours were longer. In the second century BC, the Greek astronomer Hipparchus divided the day into twenty-four equal segments.

However, keeping time was still an inexact science for the common man. Until the invention of the modern clock, just about everyone simply divided a day into twelve hours of daylight and twelve of darkness. The modern mechanical clock, which keeps time by the regulated swinging of a pendulum, was conceptualized by Galileo, the sixteenth- and seventeenth-century mathematician and philosopher. The first such timepiece was built by Dutch scientist Christiaan Huygens in the seventeenth century.

In the centuries since, clocks have become increasingly precise, culminating with invention of the atomic clock in the twentieth century. Finally, the entire population of the world is in sync. Hipparchus would be proud.

Q Why do trees lose their leaves?

A Trees that lose their leaves in the colder months are of the deciduous variety. The term "deciduous" comes from the Latin *deciduus,* which means "that which falls off." Fancy schmancy evergreens, on the other hand, get to keep their leaves all year long.

Deciduous trees lose their leaves in the winter for the same reason that bears hibernate: It's all about conserving energy. In the summer, leaves absorb nutrients from the sun; through photosynthesis, they provide the tree with energy. But as the days get shorter and there's less sunlight available, leaves suddenly become a tree's jobless friends, mooching off the tree's water supply without giving much back.

And as it turns out, these suddenly useless leaves could also pose a big safety risk for the tree during winter. Everybody's seen a tree's branches sag when they're coated with ice; if there were leaves on those branches, there would be more surface area on which frost could form and, thus, a greater chance of breakage. The additional surface area would also mean that the tree would lose more moisture to cold wind. So the tree goes naked for the winter and stores the water it needs in its trunk and branches.

But how does it happen? When the tree sets its clock back to standard time, so to speak, it begins to kick the leaves to the ground by releasing the hormones ethylene and abscisic acid. Meanwhile, two other chemical compounds—auxin and cytokinin, which are a tree's growth hormones—diminish in proportion. The leaf-dropping process continues as ethylene and abscisic acid build up a corklike material in the leaf's separation layer, which is between the leaf and the branch. The accumulation of these corky cells in the separation layer keeps any water from getting to the leaf and prevents its sugar from escaping. While the separation layer is disintegrating, a protective layer of cells forms on the tree at the leaf's base. When this process is complete, the leaf falls off. Multiply that by several hundred or thousand leaves, and you have a tree that is ready for winter.

Finally, of course, trees lose their leaves in order to provide children with giant piles to jump in. But take notice: None of these leaves are oak leaves—the separation layer of the mighty oak never deteriorates enough to allow its dead leaves to fall.

Q Why does mercury rise or fall depending on the temperature?

A It's a standard cartoon gag: The sun is beating down, eggs are frying on the sidewalk, and people are fanning themselves in overheated agony. Cut to a shot of the thermometer; mercury strains against its glass confines before blowing out the top like water from a geyser. It's exaggerated, but not as much as you may think.

Mercury expands as the temperature increases; as the temperature decreases, it contracts. (If this seems counterintuitive, it's because water reacts to temperature in the opposite way, expanding as it freezes.) As mercury expands, it is channeled upward through the thermometer's thin, hollow center; it will expand as long as the temperature continues to rise, which is why most thermometers have a reservoir at the end.

Daniel Gabriel Fahrenheit—a German glassblower, physicist, and engineer—invented the mercury thermometer in 1714. Fahrenheit chose mercury to gauge changes in temperature for two reasons:

The element is liquid at room temperature, and it expands evenly as the temperature rises. Unfortunately, mercury is also quite dangerous—even its vapors are poisonous. That's why, for the most part, digital thermometers have replaced those that are filled with mercury—there always is a chance that glass thermometers will break.

So back to the time-honored cartoon gag, from which you can learn the following lesson: If you notice eggs frying on the sidewalk, be wary of any mercury thermometers you see. Each is like a loaded gun, just waiting for the temperature to get hot enough to make it blow like a toxic Old Faithful.

Chapter Twelve

PLACES

Q Where is the most crowded place on earth?

A We know what you're thinking: The most crowded place on earth must be Disneyland on the first day of summer vacation. Or perhaps the Mall of America on the morning after Thanksgiving. Right?

Wrong. Those are anomalies, and while they might seem like hectic places at certain times, there is a section of Hong Kong that has them both beat 365 days a year. It's called Mong Kok, which translates to "flourishing/busy corner." The name is apt because, according to the *Guinness Book of World Records*, Mong Kok is the most densely populated place on the planet.

About two hundred thousand people reside in Mong Kok, an area just slightly larger than half a square mile. That's about seventy square feet per person. Add in the buildings and you've got a district in which it is physically impossible for everyone to be outside at the same time. (By comparison, the Manhattan borough of New York City is home to about 70,600 people per square mile.)

Mong Kok's bustling Golden Mile—a popular stretch of shops, restaurants, and theaters—compounds the crowding issue: A half-million or so tourists routinely jostle for position in the streets. Residents told the *New York Times* that the streets are often completely full, with every inch of pavement covered.

How is it possible to squeeze so many people into such a small area? You build up. Mong Kok is home to an array of high-rise apartment buildings. Families who live in these apartments sometimes rent out rooms to other families. There might be ten or more people in a single apartment—they sleep in two or three rooms and share a small kitchen and a single bathroom. The apartments are so small that people sleep in bunk beds that are three or four tiers high, and they keep their belongings in chests and baskets that are suspended from the ceiling.

Remember Mong Kok the next time you're elbowing your way through a crowded store on Black Friday, trying to secure the season's must-have toy. When you return home and sit at the table for dinner, at least there won't be two other families smiling back at you.

Q Has the White House always had an Oval Office?

A No. The president has always had an office in the White House, but the Oval Office itself goes back only to 1909. Before then, most chief executives worked at desks that were located in what is now the Lincoln Bedroom (on the second floor of the East Wing). Abraham Lincoln himself labored there—and his cabinet met around a solid black walnut table in the center of the room.

The White House was the largest residence in the United States when the country's second president, John Adams, moved into it in 1800. (George Washington helped to design the place but left office before it was completed.) Still, it was much smaller than it is today. In 1902, Theodore Roosevelt oversaw the construction of the West Wing and moved his office there. That space, however, was rectangular. President William Howard Taft, who was president from 1909 to 1913, was the first chief executive to work in the Oval Office. The room was positioned in the center of the West Wing, and the décor was olive green.

That, of course, was not the Oval Office we see now. A fire gutted the original in 1929, so Franklin Delano Roosevelt took the opportunity to relocate the Oval Office to the southeast corner of the West Wing. Since 1934, the room has stayed in the same place, though changes have been made to the color scheme. Roosevelt had a teal rug and dark green drapes with eagles displayed on the valences. John F. Kennedy ordered a red rug and pale curtains; in a sad twist of fate, he was assassinated on the day the old color scheme was swapped for the new.

Alert observers can date photos of the Oval Office by looking at its draperies and floor coverings. Richard Nixon went with a navy-blue carpet and gold drapes, while Gerald Ford brought in a gold rug with blue florets. In his second term, Ronald Reagan ordered a gold rug that had sunbeams radiating from its center. George H. W. Bush and Bill Clinton had different shades of blue on the floor, and George W. Bush installed a new gold sunbeam carpet (designed by First Lady Laura Bush) with gold drapes.

Yes, the look of the Oval Office has been altered over the years, but through all of the makeovers, it has remained a powerful symbol of the nation's most powerful position.

Q Who is the Martha of Martha's Vineyard?

A History contains many famous Marthas: Martha Washington, Martha Stewart, Martha Reeves (of Martha and the Vandellas), and the notorious Calamity Jane (her real name was Martha Jane Cannary).

However well known, none of these Marthas had an island named after her. That honor goes instead to a relatively unknown Martha, the mother-in-law of English explorer and colonist Bartholomew Gosnold.

In 1602, Gosnold commanded a voyage to the New World aboard the *Concord*. He reached North America at the lower coast of Maine. Continuing his exploration southward, Gosnold happened upon a peninsula, which he named Cape Cod because of the abundance of cod fish there. He also found a large, wooded island that was overflowing with luxuriant lakes, springs, and wild grapevines. He named it Martha's Vineyard in honor of his mother-in-law.

According to the Martha's Vineyard Historical Society, mother-in-law Martha may have helped finance Gosnold's New World expeditions. And chances are she was handsomely repaid. Not only did Gosnold name an island—and his infant daughter—after Martha, it's said that he returned to England with a boatload of lumber, furs, and sassafras, an aromatic North American tree that was used to make medicines, perfumes, and teas.

Gosnold probably was not the first navigator to find and name this large island off the southeastern coast of Massachusetts, but he was the first to officially record it. It helped that he had two journalists aboard the *Concord* to document his voyage.

The first Europeans to discover and visit Martha's Vineyard were the Norsemen in 1000, according to Henry Franklin Norton, author of *Martha's Vineyard: Historical, Legendary, Scenic*. The Norsemen called the island Vineland.

Also sailing past Martha's Vineyard before Gosnold was Giovanni da Verrazzano, a man of Italian descent who was a navigator and explorer for France. During his travels along the northeast coast of North America in 1524, he named the lush island in honor of another woman, Claudia, wife of France's King Francis I.

Q Has anyone jumped off the Golden Gate Bridge and lived to tell about it?

A Yes, more than two dozen people have survived the fall. That sounds like a lot—until you learn that more than 1,300 have taken the leap since the bridge opened in 1937.

With a success rate like that, the twenty-one-story drop is one of the more effective suicide methods. It's also one of the nastiest. After four seconds hurtling through the air (just enough time for a change of heart), the jumper hits the water at seventy-five miles per hour. In most cases, the force of the impact—fifteen thousand pounds per square inch—will break the jumper's ribs and vertebrae. The broken ribs usually pierce the lungs, spleen, and heart, and cause massive internal bleeding. If a jumper somehow survives, he or she likely will drown.

A handful of jumpers lived to tell the tale because they hit the water feet first. Kevin Hines jumped and survived in 2000, when he was nineteen years old. Immediately after taking the leap, he changed his mind and prayed to survive. In the rapid fall, he managed to turn himself so that he hit feet first. Hitting vertically helped Hines's body penetrate the water, reducing the force of impact. The force was great enough to break his back and shatter his vertebrae, but none of his organs were punctured. In 1979, a man survived in good enough shape—his worst injury was several cracked vertebrae—to swim ashore and drive to a hospital.

There is roughly one documented jump from the bridge every two weeks, making it the most popular suicide spot in the world. (There likely are other cases in which no one saw the jumper and the body washed out to sea.) The bridge is a jumping hotspot for two reasons: First, some people see it as romantic to leap from such a beautiful structure into the water; second, it's incredibly easy to do. The bridge has a pedestrian walkway, and all that stands between a suicidal person and the plunge is a four-foot railing. One possible explanation for this short railing is that the chief engineer of the bridge, Joseph Strauss, was only five feet tall and wanted to be able to enjoy the view.

Over the years, calls to add a barrier to the Golden Gate Bridge have been met with resistance in San Francisco. Opponents declare that the money would be better spent elsewhere; they object to compromising the beauty of the bridge to stop people from attempting suicide, since these people would likely just resort to a different method.

In October 2008, the Golden Gate Board of Directors voted to build a net system twenty feet below the bridge's platform that would catch and hold jumpers. The board then began working on raising the forty to fifty million dollars needed to install the nets. In the meantime, it's nothing but cold, hard water below.

Q How many countries have a neutralist policy?

A Bent on world domination? To an aspiring dictator, neutral countries can look like the low-hanging fruit on the tree of global conquest. They lack offensive military capabilities and they have wishy-washy foreign policies—in other words, they are there for the taking. Or so it would seem. In fact, this whole "neutral" thing is a lot more complicated than it looks.

First of all, there's a difference between being "neutral" and "neutralist." A neutralist country is one that has a policy of nonalignment: When it seems like the whole world is picking sides in an extended conflict, a neutralist country tries to stay out of it.

The neutralist movement goes back to the Cold War, to countries that refused to affiliate with either the Soviet bloc or the Western bloc of nations. India is one of the largest countries that had a neutralist policy—it tried to (ahem) curry favor with the USSR and the USA alike. But a neutralist policy doesn't mean that a country must avoid aggression. Neutralist countries have actually gone to war with each other, like Iran and Iraq did in the early 1980s.

So how many neutralist countries are there? A lot. So many that they have their own international organization, the Non-Aligned Movement (NAM), which represents most of the countries in South America, Africa, and the Middle East. And though the NAM has been called a relic of the Cold War, it's still alive and kicking.

Now, a "neutral" country is something else entirely. Neutrality is a condition that is recognized by the international laws and treaties that govern warfare. According to these agreements, when a war breaks out, disinterested countries can declare themselves neutral. This means that they have certain rights—the warring nations can't enter their territories, for example—as well as the fundamental responsibility to remain neutral by treating the warring nations impartially. Any country can potentially remain neutral during any war, as long as it can maintain that impartiality.

But this idea of limited neutrality doesn't really get to the heart of our question. We're looking for perpetually neutral countries—the Swedens and the Switzerlands of the world. Switzerland, as you may recall, has had guaranteed neutrality since the Congress of Vienna settled Napoleon's hash in 1815, and the Swedes have been neutral since about that time as well. But although Sweden stayed out of the great wars of the twentieth century, its current neutrality is debatable since it's a member of the European Union (EU) and, as such, has a stake in the EU's non-neutral foreign policy.

That leaves the Swiss. But before you start drawing up your marching orders against the soft underbelly of Switzerland, you should get familiar with the phrase "armed neutrality." This means that the Swiss aren't going to roll over for you—they've got a defensive army, or more accurately, a sort of citizen militia. Switzerland also has one of the highest gun-ownership rates in the world. So beware, aspiring dictators: This world-domination thing isn't as easy as it looks.

Q What's the deal with Young America, Minnesota?

A Some fun facts about Minnesota: Its state bird is the loon; in 1998 it elected a one-time professional wrestler as governor; and in 2008 it sent a former *Saturday Night Live* comedian to the U.S. Senate. Given these qualifiers, it's easy to believe that one of Minnesota's major export is promotional and advertising mailings.

"Go West, young man," Horace Greeley said, and in the nineteenth century, millions of Americans did. Moving into Minnesota—official beverage, milk; state motto, *L'Etoile du Nord* (The Star of the North)—they founded towns like Duluth, and in 1856, near one of the state's ten thousand lakes, they established a village that was destined for greatness.

Back then, people had faith in a thing called progress. They believed hard work and an enterprising spirit could turn just about any hamlet into a center of industry and culture. They thought that town's name ought to reflect that spirit. A catchphrase of the day, "young America," connoted the progressive and indomitable nature of the burgeoning nation. Inspired, these Minnesota settlers chose it for the name of their town.

But Young America, Minnesota, was different. Its people weren't content with duplicating the same old goods and services that emanated from other cities springing up about the Middle West. The enterprising inhabitants of Young America saw a niche—and an empty mailbox—and set about filling it.

Well, okay: Young America was in fact a farming community for much of its history. It wasn't until 1973 that it began an assault on the nation's postal arteries. That was the year a rebate processing company moved to town, changed its name from the Dile Corporation to Young America, and began sending and receiving more than two billion dollars in rebates annually. Young America—the town and the company—became the world's center for rebate processing.

To its credit, Young America, Minnesota, remains very much a small community. Fewer than four thousand people call it home, even after a 1997 merger with neighboring Norwood that formed a burg that's officially known as Norwood Young America. And each day, the dream of those early settlers is manifest in the two-dollar checks that sally forth to flood the nation's mailboxes.

Indeed, it seems to be a role that Young America was destined to play, for its earliest established institution was a post office.

Q What's the difference between England and Britain?

A In either case, we're talking about those two islands just off the northwest coast of the main European landmass. There's a bunch of smaller islands out there, but the ones we need to focus on are Great Britain and Ireland. Great Britain is home to three countries: England, Scotland, and Wales. Ireland is home to Northern Ireland and the Republic of Ireland. So that's five countries between two islands.

Now, England, Scotland, Wales, and Northern Ireland make up what's known as the United Kingdom of Great Britain and Northern Ireland, or the United Kingdom for short. The United Kingdom is also often referred to as the UK or—and here's the kicker—Britain. So Britain, or the UK, spreads out over a couple of large islands, as well as some of those smaller ones we mentioned earlier. London is the capital of England and the UK, and its people are called English; Scotland's capital is Edinburgh and its people are referred to as Scottish; the capital of Wales is Cardiff and its people are called Welsh; and Northern Ireland's capital is Belfast and its people are referred to as Irish.

What everyone knows as Britain is actually a union of these four countries. England is simply one of the countries in that union, and you shouldn't use England to describe the UK, although you can refer to people from the UK as British. Another no-no is lumping the Republic of Ireland in with the UK. The Republic of Ireland gained its independence from the UK in 1922 and fiercely defends this status.

So ends our tutorial on those islands across the pond. Now you can have a conversation with anyone from these countries without the fear that you'll make a complete idiot out of yourself.

Q Why do so many country names end in "-stan"?

A No, there was no Stan the Conqueror running around founding countries in ancient times. The real answer is a lot less exciting. There are "-stan" countries for the same reason there are "-land" countries—*stan* is an old Persian word meaning "place," "land," or "home." As people from ancient Persia (modern-day Iran) spread to different areas of western Asia, they took the suffix with them.

Today, there are seven independent "-stan" nations in central Asia (including some that creep over into Eastern Europe); five were formerly republics of the Soviet Union. There are also three "-stan" republics in the Russian Federation, three "-stan" provinces in Iran, and several historical "-stan" regions in various Asian countries.

Typically, place names formed with "-stan" describe a land in terms of its inhabitants. For example, Afghanistan means "land of the Afghans." In other cases, "-stan" formations evoke the landscape itself, like the name Dagestan (a Russian republic), which means "land of the mountains."

Pakistan is a recent addition to the "-stan" list. In 1930, the Muslim philosopher Sir Muhammad Iqbal called for a new Muslim state to be carved out of what was then British India. Students who supported the idea proposed calling the new country Pakistan for its double meaning. It literally meant "land of the pure" *(pak)*, and according to Peter Blood's book *Pakistan: A Country Study,* it also incorporated letters from some of the predominantly Muslim regions in the area—**P**unjab, **A**fghania, **K**ashmir, **I**ran, **S**indh, **T**ukharistan, Afgha**n**istan, and Balochis**tan**.

Just think—if Persians had discovered the New World, we might all be living in the United States of Americastan.

Q Are there really no snakes in Ireland?

A Snakes have never set foot, er, slithered into Ireland, so it's not true that Saint Patrick rid the country of the scaly reptiles by driving them into a sea of green beer.

Initially, what is now known as Ireland lacked a climate that was warm enough to accommodate snakes. About eighty-five hundred years ago, temperatures rose enough to make Ireland a nice home for slitherers, but it wasn't to be. The veritable heat wave melted the ice that connected Ireland to Europe, and it became the island that it is today. Talk about the luck of the Irish: Since it was surrounded by water, it was beyond the reach of those scary snakes.

So why does Great Britain, Ireland's closest neighbor and also an island, have snakes? Great Britain was connected to Europe until about sixty-five hundred years ago. Three species of snakes made it to Great Britain before the melting glaciers created the English Channel and isolated it from the mainland. Great Britain is as far as the snakes got—by then, Ireland was an island.

In addition to lacking snakes, Ireland has only one species of lizard, frog, toad, and newt. In the 1960s, humans introduced the "slow worm," a legless lizard that some mistake for a snake, into the wild.

What about the legend of Saint Patrick driving the snakes from Ireland ? Well, as anyone who majored in English in college knows, allegory is a powerful form of storytelling. In the case of Saint Patrick, snakes might have represented pagans as he worked tirelessly to convert people to Christianity.

If you really hate snakes, you'll be heartened to learn that Ireland isn't the only place on the planet without them. New Zealand, Iceland, Greenland, and Antarctica are also snake-free.

Q Is there a fountain of youth?

A Juan Ponce de León allegedly thought so. The Spanish explorer was supposedly searching for the fabled fountain when he discovered Florida. However, it wasn't until after his death in 1521 that he became linked with the fountain.

The first published reference associating Ponce de León with the fountain of youth was the *Historia General y Natural de las Indias,* by Gonzalo Fernandez de Oviedo in 1535. The author cited the explorer's search for a fountain of restorative water to cure his impotence, but the veracity of this account is questionable since Ponce de León had children at the time of his 1513 voyage and didn't even mention the fountain in his travel notes.

Moreover, the fountain of youth legend predates Ponce de León. In Arabic versions of the *Alexander Romance,* a collection of myths about Alexander the Great, the Macedonian king and his troops cross a desert and come to a fountain in which they bathe to regain strength and youth. This story was translated to French in the thirteenth century and was well known among Europeans.

If a fountain of youth actually exists, no one has found it in it in any of its supposed locations, which are most typically cited as Florida, the Bahamas, or the Bay of Honduras. It may turn out, however, that a fountain of youth exists in science. David Sinclair, a Harvard University professor and the founder of Sirtris Pharmaceuticals, discovered that the molecule resveratrol could extend the lifespan of worms and fruit flies in 2003. In 2006, Italian researchers prolonged the life of the fish *Nothobranchius furzeri* with resveratrol.

Drugs that are based on this research are in clinical trials and could be on shelves soon, though initially they will be designed only to aid diabetics. It's not quite eternal life—it's basically just extended fitness. But that's more than Ponce de León found.

Q Why isn't Scotland Yard in Scotland?

A British nomenclature is loaded with misleading terms. Plum pudding is not pudding, nor does it contain plums. Real tennis doesn't have much to do with real tennis. Spotted dick is not a venereal disease, but rather a delicious dessert—a dish that thankfully has nothing to do with what you might think. Given this legacy of verbal imprecision, it's perhaps not surprising that the headquarters of the famous police force that patrols London is called Scotland Yard.

It started in 1829, when Charles Rowan and Richard Mayne were charged with organizing a citywide crime-fighting force. At the time the two men lived together in a house at 4 Whitehall Place, and they ran their fledgling outfit out of their garage, using the back courtyard as a makeshift police station. "Rowan and Mayne's Backyard" wasn't an appropriate name for the headquarters of a police force. Instead, it was called Scotland Yard. Why? London police don't play bagpipes; haggis isn't part of the rations; and as far as we know, London policemen don't wear kilts (at least not in public). So what gives?

You might think that a mystery like this would be a perfect case for Scotland Yard. Unfortunately, those famed investigators aren't sure how their hallowed institution got its name, which is not necessarily a compelling endorsement of their detective work. After years of research, though, word detectives have narrowed the origin of the name to two likely possibilities.

According to the first explanation, Scotland Yard sits on the location of what was once the property of Scottish royalty. The story goes that back before Scotland and England unified in 1707, the present-day Scotland Yard was a residence used by Scottish kings and ambassadors when they visited London on diplomatic sojourns. The other, less regal possibility is that 4 Whitehall Place backed onto a courtyard called Great Scotland Yard, named for the medieval landowner—Scott—who owned the property.

Regardless of the name's true origin, the Metropolitan police have moved on—sort of. In 1890 they decided that they needed new digs and moved to a larger building on the Victoria Embankment. Given a chance to redeem themselves and give their headquarters a name that actually made sense, what did the London police choose? New Scotland Yard.

Q What are the requirements to be a country?

A Considering the amount of time we spend celebrating global diversity, you'd think that we could all agree on some basic facts about the world—like the number of countries that there are. But no—depending on whom you ask, there are as few as 192 or as many as 260.

Part of the problem is that there's no official rulebook that explains exactly what it takes to be a country. And we certainly can't just take any would-be country's word for it—otherwise those gun-toting survivalists in northern Idaho might have a point about seceding from the Union. In fact, if you think about it, it's kind of hard to define what exactly a country is. The word "country" can evoke a landscape, the people who live on it, or the laws that govern them there—and often it conjures all of those things. The concept of countryhood is one of those ideas that we take for granted but struggle to articulate.

Fortunately, the lawyers of the world have got our backs. International laws can work only if the requirements of countryhood are well defined. One influential legal definition of a country is spelled out in the Montevideo Convention on the Rights and Duties of States, a treaty that was signed by North and South American nations in Montevideo, Uruguay, in 1933. In Article I, it says: "The state as a person of international law should possess the following qualifications: (a) a permanent population; (b) a defined territory; (c) government; and (d) capacity to enter into relations with the other states."

Article III of the treaty makes it clear that any group that meets these four requirements has the right to become a country, even if other countries refuse to recognize it as such. This was an innovation. In earlier times, becoming a country was more like joining an exclusive club: You had to impress the most popular members—namely, the nations that dominated the world with their wealth and military power—and convince them to let you in. Their opinion was the only thing that mattered.

But even under the newer egalitarian rules, there's a loophole that keeps the global "country club" more exclusive than it might seem. According to the Montevideo definition, you need to have "the capacity to enter into relations with other states," which effectively means that other states have to agree to enter into relations with you. In other words, you still have to get at least one country to recognize you, even if you fulfill the other requirements for automatic statehood.

So how do established countries decide which hopefuls they choose to recognize? In practice, it often comes down to political expediency. Taiwan, for example, looks like it fulfills all of the requirements of statehood that are laid out by the Montevideo Convention. But many countries—the United States included—haven't recognized Taiwan as an independent state, because the Chinese, who think of Taiwan as part of their own territory, would be royally pissed.

There you have it. In practice, fully recognized countryhood comes down to who you know, just like virtually everything else in this world.

Q How much rain does it take to make a rain forest?

A It takes eighty inches of rain per year to make a rain forest, but the scientists who categorize these things aren't picky. There should be no feelings of inadequacy among forests whose drops per annum don't quite make the cut; if a wooded area has a rate of precipitation that comes close to the eighty-inch mark, it will gladly be taken into the fold.

Rain falls about ninety days per year in a rain forest. As much as 50 percent of this precipitation evaporates, meaning that rain forests recycle their water supply. In non-rain forest areas, water evaporates and is transported (via clouds) to different regions. In a rain forest, however, the unique climate and weather patterns often cause the precipitation to fall over the same area from which it evaporated.

A rain forest is comprised of evergreen trees, either broadleaf or coniferous, and other types of intense vegetation—these regions collectively contain more than two-thirds of the plant species on the planet. There are two types of rain forests: tropical and temperate. Tropical rain forests are located near the equator; temperate rain forests crop up near oceanic coastlines, particularly where mountain ranges focus rainfall on a particular region.

Rain forests can be found on every continent except Antarctica. The largest tropical rain forest is the Amazon in South America; the largest temperate rain forest is in the Pacific Northwest, stretching from northern California all the way to Alaska.

At one time, rain forests covered as much as 14 percent of the earth, but that number is now down to about 6 percent. Scientists estimate that an acre and a half of rain forest—the equivalent of a little more than a football field—is lost every second. The trees are taken for lumber, and the land is tilled for farming. At that rate, scientists estimate, rain forests will disappear completely within the next forty years—and it will take a lot more than eighty inches of rain per year to bring them back.

Q Where is the world's worst place to live?

A The worst place to live, much like beauty, is in the eye of the beholder. If you enjoy long hikes in untrammeled countryside, then the megalopolis Tokyo would probably be a bad match for you. Similarly, if you enjoy the rich culture of a big city, a life spent in Maza, North Dakota (2007 population: four), might seem akin to burning in hell. If you wake up each morning to find that your ex has again slashed your car tires and left a flaming sack of solid waste on your doorstep, then the town in which you reside is most likely the worst place in the world to live.

When serious types sit down to make their worst-cities-in-the-world lists, they usually look at quantifiable measures such as pollution or infant mortality rate. *Popular Science* magazine, for instance, placed Pittsburgh, Pennsylvania, on its list of the world's ten worst cities because of its toxic air quality. Sure, the 'Burgh could stand to learn a thing or two about going green, but take in a baseball game at beautiful PNC Park and head over to Primanti Brothers for a pastrami and cheese, and then try to say it's a terrible place to live.

Another factor that many "worst" lists point to is war. Makes sense. The likelihood of getting killed simply by walking out your front door is a flaw that most prospective homeowners would be unable to overlook. Popular choices in this category feature any number of cities in the war-torn Congo and, of course, Baghdad, Iraq. But bad wars can happen to good cities. There have been a number of violent conflicts in Paris, but most people will agree that the City of Lights has rebounded nicely.

If only there was a city that could bring it all together—a city that could take the constant threat of violence, mix in government corruption, and top it off with squalid living conditions. Well, *The Economist* found just such a place. After reviewing 130 world capitals, the magazine declared that Port Moresby, the capital of Papua New Guinea, is the world's worst place to live. Port Moresby has exceptionally high rates of murder and rape, massive unemployment, and no welfare system.

This sounds horrendous, but remember, it was a survey of only world capitals. Surely there's some off-the-map hellhole that makes Port Moresby look like Aspen. We'll keep looking, but in the meantime Port Moresby is the champ.

Q Why is Kansas City in Missouri and Missouri City in Texas?

A In the vast expanse that is the United States, there are quite a few cities and towns that have the names of outside states. How about Virginia City, Nevada; Colorado City, Arizona; and Michigan City, Indiana? Pretty unimaginative—and confusing—huh?

In the case of Kansas City, Missouri, the town officially claimed the Kansas name before the state of Kansas existed. In 1838, John Calvin McCoy, who is regarded as the father of Kansas City, and thirteen other men bought 271 acres of land that was then known as the Gabriel Prudhomme farm. This property would become Kansas City's first downtown district, but first the men needed to agree on a name for their new township. According to legend, the owners considered several names, including Port Fonda, Rabbitville, and Possum Trot. In the end, they settled on Kansas, for the Kansa Indians who inhabited the area.

Kansas, Missouri, was chartered as a town on June 1, 1850, and as a city on February 22, 1853. In 1854, the Kansas-Nebraska Act established the boundaries of a large territory to the west, which was also given the name Kansas. The territory of Kansas became the thirty-fourth state in 1861. In 1889, the Missouri city known as Kansas officially changed its name to Kansas City to distinguish itself from the Kansas the state.

As for how Missouri City came to be in Texas, that was a matter of marketing. In 1890, real-estate developers from Houston bought four acres of land near the BBB&C railroad. In an effort to draw settlers from the north to their new railroad, farming, and ranching town, the developers named the area Missouri City and launched an advertising campaign in St. Louis, Missouri.

Missouri City was touted as "a land of genial sunshine and eternal summer." Despite the developers' appeals to the residents of the Show-Me state, most of Missouri City's initial settlers came from Arlington, Texas. When a wave of settlers from the north did make it down to Missouri City the following year, they were greeted by a harsh blizzard that included twenty-eight inches of snow.

Q If you lived in Siberia and ticked off the Russian government, where would you be sent?

A The frozen and desolate expanse of Siberia is infamous as a place of forced exile for Russian political dissidents. But if you already lived in Siberia and ran afoul of the authorities, where would you be sent? Possibly to a prison elsewhere in Russia, and anywhere would likely be better than Siberia.

Russia is the world's largest country by landmass, and Siberia accounts for more than 75 percent of it—it's about 5.2 million square miles. Until very recently, large areas of Siberia were difficult to get to . . . and, thus, difficult to escape from. This made it an ideal place to send those who questioned Russian authority. The Russian government started banishing people to distant parts of the country—not just Siberia—around the seventeenth century, and it continued to do so until after World War II.

Political and criminal exiles were sent to Siberian labor camps known as gulags. Many of these gulags were in remote areas in northeast Siberia. Sevvostlag, a system of labor camps, was set up in the Kolyma region, within the Arctic Circle. Parts of the Kolyma mountain range weren't even discovered until 1926. It's a land of permafrost and tundra, with six-month-long winters during which the average temperature range is –2 degrees to –36 degrees Fahrenheit. Northeastern Siberia is home to the coldest town on the planet, Oymyakon, which once recorded a low of –96.2.

Siberia's first settlements were established relatively late in Russia's history, around the seventeenth century, but the region now supports several cities of more than half a million people. These are situated mostly in the south and have been accessible by rail since the early twentieth century. The storied Trans-Siberian Railway runs from Moscow east to Vladivostok, a distance of about 5,800 miles. The workforce that built the railway consisted of soldiers and, yes, labor-camp inmates.

Chapter Thirteen

MORE GOOD STUFF

Q Why does flashing your middle finger mean "[bleep] you"?

A The answer to this is easy; the answer to "Who did it first?" is nigh on impossible. But since we enjoy a challenge, we'll give you a two-for-one deal and tackle both questions.

Making a gesture with your middle finger is to swearing what the words "pop," "fart," and "click" are to their respective meanings. Those words sound like what they mean, and "the finger" looks like what it means.

When you consider that humans gesture all day long with their hands and fingers, that the idea embodied in the phrase "[bleep] you" is among the most primal human emotions, and that the middle finger is the longest and therefore most noticeable of all the digits, it's almost impossible to imagine a world without "the finger." Humans either would have to be devoid of anger or cloven of hoof not to have developed the gesture. It's us. That's why there's "the finger."

Now, unless your house is on fire and you're busy closing this book, you're probably wondering who exactly invented "the finger." As we said, no one knows for sure. We're going to guess that some very early, hairy human did it, sticking to our claim that the gesture requires only a caveman's awareness of three things: sexual power, the middle finger, and metaphor.

The first-known written references to "the finger" came from comic writers in ancient Greece and Rome. The Greek comic Aristophanes refers to a middle-finger insult in his play *The Clouds* (423 BC), and the Roman poet Martial does the same in works written a little more than five hundred years later.

Today, variations of "the finger"—different motions, different angles of orientation, different groups of fingers, using the thumb, etc.—are found around the world. It's a universal gesture. In all of its incarnations, "the finger" pretty much says it all.

Q Why isn't anyone ever smiling in old photographs?

A To hear the older generation tell it, the world used to be a bleak, severe place. There were no televisions, no telephones, no automobiles. Dinner was a crust of bread, and chores took twenty hours a day. The wind was always gusting, the temperature was perpetually forty below, and the only direction that existed was uphill. And based on old photographs, everybody was apparently ticked off all the time.

For many years, portrait photography was a grim business. Look at almost any portrait photo from the nineteenth century—the subjects are bound to be glaring back at you, usually while in ridiculous poses and surrounded by all sorts of odd props. Part of the reason for this pomp and circumstance was that photography was a new technology at the time, but portraiture was not. Classically, portraits were never painted of a smiling subject. For one thing, it would be physically impossible to hold a smile for the hours it took to complete a painted portrait. But it was also considered silly or ignoble to be depicted with a smile. Most people who commissioned portraits of themselves wanted to be portrayed as serious and fair-minded, great leaders of men—not as drunken court jesters.

When photographic portraits became the rage in the mid-nineteenth century, photographers and subjects maintained the tradition of somber regality. However, tradition was only part of it. There were physical limits, as well: Exposure times of early cameras could be up to several minutes. Pretending to smile for more than a minute or so becomes awfully tough on the facial muscles, as anyone who's suffered through a dinner with future in-laws can attest.

As camera technology improved and exposure times decreased, there was no longer any physical reason for portrait subjects not to smile. Still, the convention lived on in many photographers' studios, which is why there were unsmiling photographed subjects well into the twentieth century.

People who study the history of photography point to George Eastman as one of the major forces behind putting the smile into photographed portraits. Eastman, the founder of Kodak, is credited with inventing the roll of film and popularizing snapshot photography among the public, and his early advertisements helped turn photography from a serious pastime into a fun-for-the-whole-family hobby.

Although people didn't smile in old photographs, it wasn't necessarily because they were angry at the world. But you couldn't blame them if they were. Can you imagine living your life in black and white?

Q Why can't you get directory assistance for cell phone numbers?

A What's the matter? Not getting enough dinner-hour sales pitches from telemarketers or 2:00 AM ramblings from a drunken ex?

As people abandon landline phones in favor of the wireless variety, it has become increasingly difficult to track down phone numbers that aren't listed in our personal address books. For many of us, this newfound privacy is a good thing.

But privacy is an unintended offshoot of the cell-phone revolution. The main reason that there's no directory assistance for cell phones is because the wireless business is made up of so many companies. Back in the days of the monolithic Bell System, it was easy to compile a list of all customers and their phone numbers and make them available. But with so many competing cell-phone carriers, it became impossible to produce a similarly comprehensive, up-to-date database.

There is a movement afoot to change this. In 2004, five of the biggest wireless carriers—Alltel, Cingular Wireless (now AT&T), Nextel Communications, Sprint PCS, and T-Mobile USA—banded together to work toward compiling a directory-assistance database of cell phone numbers. There are a couple of problems with this plan. First, did you notice any significant omissions from that list of companies? That's right—Verizon Wireless, which had the most subscribers of any U.S. carrier when this idea was hatched, chose not to participate. Second, there's the issue of privacy—a whole lot of people would go a whole lot of nuts if their cell-phone numbers were published for public consumption.

Proponents of cell-phone directory assistance say you won't need to worry about privacy. They point out that you will have the option to keep your number unlisted, just as with landline numbers. And Federal Communications Commission regulations already prohibit most telemarketing calls to cell and landline phones.

Either way, you may not need to worry about this for a while. Work on the cell-phone directory assistance plan is taking so long that it makes the wait on hold for your wireless carrier's customer service department seem like a walk in the park.

Q Which is the loudest rock band ever?

A This question is momentous to anyone with a shred of rock and roll DNA, and right now the answer is open to dispute. The *Guinness Book of World Records* no longer keeps official records in this category, apparently not wanting to encourage people to do permanent damage to their ears. The most recent claim was made by the English hardcore band Gallows in 2007, after they hooked twelve amps and twelve speaker cabinets together in a studio and reportedly pumped out 132.5 decibels of noise, which is louder than the sound you would hear standing next to a jet engine.

The band had to wear earplugs and the heavy ear covers that airline employees use on the tarmac. "You could feel the sound blasting through the amps. It was [bleeping] off the hook!" Gallows guitarist Laurent Bernard told the music magazine *Kerrang!* "More importantly, that's louder than [previous purported record holder] Manowar. I am louder than Manowar! That's all I care about!"

It's nice to have such clear goals in life.

Manowar, the bombastic U.S. metal band, claimed 129.5 decibels in 1994. This was an unofficial addendum to its *Guinness* record of loudest musical performance from 1984. Not to run down Gallows or Manowar, but the loudness record has clearly fallen into the hands of lesser

lights in the past generation. Previous *Guinness*-approved record holders included The Who, Deep Purple, The Rolling Stones, and Kiss—a veritable smorgasbord of rock icons.

The Who has the added distinction of having blown up its own drum kit with a concussion bomb, on *The Smothers Brothers Comedy Hour* television show in 1967. Some cite this incident as the origin of guitarist Pete Townshend's impaired hearing, but he blames it on too much loud music through headphones in the recording studio.

Anyhow, while the answer to this question lacks certainty right now, it resonates—so to speak—with headbangers of all ages. In fact, it brings up a related question that's just as significant: What was the loudest concert you ever attended? Can you still feel your head vibrating? If so, Gallows would be proud.

Q Why does the U.S. government think you need to be twenty-one to buy a beer but only eighteen to buy a gun?

A The United States has some strange laws. In one Illinois town, you can't give a lit cigar to a domesticated animal. In Marshalltown, Iowa, horses are prohibited from eating fire hydrants. In Gary, Indiana, it is illegal to go to a theater or opera house within four hours of eating garlic. (Of course, this would entail finding a theater or opera house in Gary.) But perhaps the most incongruous laws are two that are shared by just about every state: You have to be twenty-one to legally buy a beer, but only eighteen to purchase a lethal weapon.

The history of the United States is filled with moral righteousness. This can largely be traced back to the Puritans who came over from England seeking to build their morally perfect "city on a hill." The influence of these dour settlers has resonated for centuries in the form of highly restrictive legal codes, like the ill-advised experiment with Prohibition in the 1920s and 1930s. When Prohibition was overturned, most state leaders compromised with their teetotaling voters and set the drinking age at twenty-one.

Guns have been subject to much less regulation than alcohol over the course of U.S. history, in part because the founding fathers decided that everyone should have the right to bear one—or at least to carry one while serving in a militia, depending on whom you ask. Indeed, it wasn't until the Gun Control of Act of 1968 that there was even an age limit for purchasing guns by mail—eighteen for rifles and twenty-one for handguns. And as every patriotic red-blooded American knows, you only need to be eighteen to enlist in the United States military.

The legal drinking and gun-owning ages were on a collision course during the Vietnam War, when young Americans who had been, drafted into a war that many of them didn't want to fight, pointed out that it seemed illogical for the government to trust an eighteen-year-old soldier to handle an M-16 in a foreign land but not a beer at the local tavern. Partially as a result of this, many states experimented with lowering the drinking age, some to as low as eighteen years old.

Makes sense, right? Wrong. In this case, the government had been right in the first place—or so the numbers seem to indicate. Study after study has shown that lowering the drinking age increased alcohol-related traffic accidents. As a result, the brief experiment ended, and today all fifty states require drinkers to be at least twenty-one years old.

Regardless of age limits, guns and alcohol never mix. In 1997, a drunken young Florida man entered a Kmart to purchase a rifle. The fact that he was so drunk that he needed a clerk to help him fill out the paperwork didn't faze store employees. It should have: The man left the store and shot his ex-girlfriend, leaving her paralyzed. But hey, at least he didn't imitate an animal while buying the gun—in Miami, that's against the law.

Q Why do we wash bath towels if we're clean when we use them?

A You may think that you're dirt-free after a bath or a shower, but the human body is never truly clean. Your skin supports a host of icky things—such as yeast and bacteria—and your bath towel absorbs them when you're drying yourself. Furthermore, a lot of your surface skin is made up of dead skin cells, which cling to you unless they're scraped off by an abrasive object such as a towel or a brush: This gunk collects in your towel. The air around you in your home also contains dead skin, dirt, microscopic bits of dead bugs, and other debris. So even when your towel is innocently hanging from its hook, it's getting dirty.

By the way, if your towels continue to have a musty smell after you launder them, it might be due to mildew in your washing machine. Your washer may retain water, which stagnates and results in mildew. Because bath towels are so absorbent, they're more obviously affected than other items.

So give your washing machine the once-over and toss your towels in there on a regular basis. Staying clean is a never-ending battle.

Q Who was Jerry, and why was he so good at rigging things?

A To be precise, Jerry never rigged things; he built them. "Jerry-rig" is a conjunction of two separate and unequal phrases—"jury-rig" and "jerry-built"—and making the distinction is important if you want to keep your meaning clear.

The older of the two terms, "jury-rig," makes reference to a ship's mast. "Jury" is a nautical term for a replacement mast, while "rig" refers to the ropes, pulleys, sails, and other miscellany that make the ship go. Performing a jury-rig literally means replacing a broken mast with a new one.

The other phrase has less definable origins. Some believe that it's a reference to the Biblical city of Jericho. The story goes that a troop of marching soldiers knocked down the city's walls by circling it a number of times and blowing horns. Thus, a jerry-built structure is one that is prone to collapsing under very little strain.

The two phrases imply different levels of craftsmanship. A jury-rig is done at sea, sometimes in adverse conditions, and the replacement mast has to be good enough to get the crew home. It's not a task to be taken lightly.

Jerry-built, on the other hand, refers to anything that's shoddily put together, using whatever tools and materials are handy. In nine-

teenth-century England, a jerry-builder was someone who constructed flimsy houses with cheap materials. Quick and dirty was,
and is, the jerry-builder's way.

So it's really quite simple: Jerry-built equals bad, jury-rig equals
good. Confuse the two terms at your own peril.

Q Why do radio and TV station call letters begin with W or K?

A The reason goes back nearly a hundred years, before the
Titanic sailed or World War I was fought. In the early
twentieth century, radio was a form of communication rather
than entertainment. Radio, or "wireless telephony," was used to
send messages from ship to shore and station to station. (The
idea of broadcasting music to masses of people didn't catch on
until the 1920s.)

Back then, every telegraph station had a code to identify it, and
those code letters were appended to every message a station sent
out. The first radio operators used telegraphic codes as well, so
they adopted the practice of using "calls," or call letters, to quickly
identify themselves to each other.

In 1912, the United States Bureau of Navigation standardized the
practice and took over the duty of assigning call letters. There were
so few stations—some on land, some on ships—that a three-letter
designation could cover all of them. An international agreement
assigned the first letter of each call sign to different countries. The
United States got the letters N and W, as well as part of the Ks:

KDA through KZZ. (Germany had KAA through KCZ, though all the Ks were reassigned to the United States in 1929.)

The United States used N to designate government stations. K was for stations on the Pacific coast and for ships in the Gulf of Mexico and the Atlantic Ocean. Originally, W was for ships on the Pacific Ocean and Great Lakes and for land stations on the East Coast. Sound confusing? Of course it was; the government was involved. To further muddle matters, the Panama Canal allowed ships to travel between the Pacific and Atlantic Oceans, so their call-sign designations became meaningless.

Then radio became an entertainment industry rather than simply a messaging system. In the 1920s, radio exploded in popularity, and call signs were expanded to four letters instead of three in order to cover all the new stations. And that was just AM radio.

When FM radio and television stations were added to the mix, the Federal Communication Commission decided to stay with the K and W. It simply added an FM or TV to the end. When some stations folded, their call letters were reassigned to new ones. Old habits may not be terribly efficient, but they die hard.

Q Why is a face called a mug?

A "Mug" is one of those terms that rarely is used in normal conversation—except when we're referring to pro athletes and Hollywood bad boys, whose mug shots frequently appear on the nightly news.

Still, most of us don't need newscast reminders to know that a mug is a face—and often an ugly one at that. This is because we've watched *The Three Stooges* and all of those films from the first half of the twentieth century that seem to have their own unique vernacular. For instance, a normal person might say, "I had some competition getting the attention of a woman." But in Old-Time Movieland language, this is spoken as, "Say, I got into a scrape with some palooka over a dame. A real wise guy. Why, I socked him right in his ugly mug!" (These words are uttered with a Brooklyn accent, regardless of whether the conversation is taking place in New York, Milwaukee, Atlanta, Mexico City, or ancient Rome; in Old-Time Movieland, everybody sounds like William Bendix.)

"Mug" predates Old-Time Movieland, though. It's been used as a noun to describe the face and as a verb for the word "grimace" since the seventeenth century. It likely derives from *mugg,* a Scandinavian word for a drinking vessel. In the seventeenth and eighteenth centuries, mugs were often decorated with cartoon-ishly drawn human faces, which may have led to the use of "mug" as a synonym for an ugly face. Another theory is that "mug" comes from *mukha,* a Sanskrit word for face. We have yet to determine, however, whether Sanskrit was spoken with a Brooklyn accent.

Q Why are reflections in a mirror reversed?

A When you look at your reflection, you see a person with the same top and bottom as you. The head and bejeweled tiara are up high, and the feet and cowboy boots are down low. But when you raise your right hand, your reflection raises its left hand. When you pick your left nostril, your reflection picks its right. Is the man in the mirror just being contrary? Why does the mirror flip things left to right but not up to down?

Simply put, it doesn't—a mirror doesn't flip things left to right. A mirror only reverses in and out—depth—while leaving everything else intact. But as you'll discover, the depth inversion fools your brain into thinking that it's really left and right that get switched.

You can envision this depth inversion more clearly when you see a reflecting surface from an angle other than straight-on. Imagine an idyllic nature scene—a happy little tree reflected in a lake. When you compare the real tree to its reflection, you'll notice that the right-hand branches of the real tree show up on the right-hand side of the reflected tree—it's just that the reflection is upside down, inverted. It's almost as if somebody grabbed the top of the tree and pulled it straight down, through the trunk, the way you would invert a reversible poncho.

Now imagine, as you look into the mirror, that somebody did the same thing to you. (Ouch!) This is essentially what your reflection is—a version of you with your depth, relative to the mirror, perfectly inverted. So why does it seem like left and right are switched? When you stand to the side of a mirror and watch someone looking at his or her reflection, the relationship between the real person and the inverted image is clear, because you've got a good view of both. But when you're gazing lovingly at your own reflection, it's not as obvious. Your reflection looks a lot like you, not like the horrible, depth-inverted freak that it is. So instead of thinking of the reflection's right hand as an inverted version of your right hand, you imagine yourself standing as the reflection is standing—and you think of your reflected right hand as a left hand.

You can see that this is the case with a simple thought experiment. Imagine you're facing north and looking into a mirror. Point east and your reflection points east. Point up and your reflection points up. But point north—toward the mirror—and your reflection points right back out at you—south. It's only in and out that are flipped.

Now stop staring at your reflection and give somebody else a chance, you freakin' narcissist.

Q Why do airplane seats need to be "fully upright" for takeoff and landing?

A You're taking the red-eye home from vacation so you can get to work on time the next morning. Minutes into the flight, you have a pillow tucked under your head and your seat reclined in just the right position—you're dozing before the twinkling lights on the ground have even faded to black. Before you know it, the flight attendant is telling you that the plane will be landing shortly and that you need to return your seat to the standard upright position. You don't remember asking for the complimentary wake-up call, so why are you being pestered?

As is the case with many of life's minor irritations, the underlying concept here is safety. The Federal Aviation Administration (FAA) requires that all seats be in the standard upright and locked position immediately prior to the takeoff and landing of a commercial airliner. Which is why, when you ask for five more minutes, the flight attendant doesn't let you roll over and go back to sleep. The idea is that most emergency situations occur as a plane is preparing for takeoff or coming in for a landing. If disaster strikes, the FAA wants each passenger to have as clear a route to the emergency exits as possible.

In economy class, the average seat "pitch" (the distance between a point on your seat and the same point on the seat directly behind or in front of you) is between thirty-one and thirty-four inches. That's not much real estate. A reclined seat drastically reduces the freedom of movement of the passenger behind you. Add an open tray table to the mix, and the escape route begins to resemble an obstacle course. (Seats in the row in front of the emergency exits don't recline, allowing for better access in case of emergency.)

So the next time you've muffled the flight attendant's voice by holding your pillow over your ears, mistaken her nose for the snooze button on your alarm clock, and told yourself that it's only a dream and that you're still in your five-star hotel room, try to shake yourself awake and follow the poor woman's instructions. After that, apologize for batting her nose. Then avoid making eye contact with her for the rest of the flight.

Q Why do Brits lose their accents when they sing?

A Partly because they have to, but mostly because they want to. As to the "have to," linguists say that in order to project your voice, you have to open your mouth a little wider, and this has the effect of neutralizing some of the vowel tones that are key to any accent. Thus, the voice is regularized in a way that isn't specifically American, but does eliminate some of the qualities that characterize an accent.

As to the "want to," consider that you can find many pop singers who "lose" their accents. It's because they want to sound more authentic to the styles of music that they're adopting. Take that fabulous mess of a genius, Amy Winehouse—she has such a thick North London accent when she talks that she's almost unintelligible to Americans, but when she sings, she sounds uncannily like a black soul diva. Folks say that U2's Bono, an Irishman, usually sounds quite American—maybe because he sometimes emulates Van Morrison, another Irishman, who often sounds American because his music draws so heavily from American blues and soul.

Sometimes the Beatles sound British, sometimes American. On *Abbey Road*'s unforgettable ditty "Her Majesty," Paul McCartney comes off as plenty British—he's claiming to be in love with the Queen. On *The White Album,* John Lennon sounds fairly American on the grungy blues tune "Yer Blues"—reportedly, he was mocking the British blues scene with its Yank pretensions. On the same album, McCartney is unmistakably British on the delta-inspired "Revolution 1," such as when he pronounces "evolution" with the long "e" in the first syllable.

Want more proof that singers can control their accents? The Proclaimers, a popular Scottish folk-rock duo from the late 1980s and 1990s, had brogues as thick as fog—no sounding American for them, because it would have diminished their fresh-faced, folksy appeal. Current pop diva Lily Allen purposely sounds every bit the Londoner on her tunes—and draws barbs from some who say it makes her seem trite.

The same type of criticism is aimed at Green Day, though in reverse. The members of this American pop-punk band have a vaguely British sound to their voices, probably in homage to—or simply in imitation of—the British groups that started the punk revolution. The upshot is that singers cop the inflections that seem to suit the genre they're in or even the individual tune they're performing. Be attuned to that, and you'll enjoy pop music even more, mate.

Q Why doesn't the United States use the metric system?

A For many Americans who have driven into Canada, the most immediately noticeable difference is the way things are measured. Distances are shown in kilometers and gas is sold by the liter, which can be confusing when you're used to miles and gallons. American travelers in Europe, or pretty much anywhere else in the world, face the same problem. Why does the United States stubbornly cling to its own idiosyncratic system of weights and measures when the metric system is easier to use and universally recognized? Liberia and Myanmar are the world's only other countries that have not adopted the metric system.

Well, this turns out to be a bit of a trick question, because in many ways the United States *has* adopted the metric system. An 1866 law made it legal to use metric measurements in contracts and agreements. In 1893, the United States set the official definitions of U.S. units based on metric units—one U.S. pound equals 453.59237 grams, for example. And the Metric Conversion Act of 1975 (among several other laws passed over the decades) encouraged the adoption of metric units by American science and industry. For the most part, American scientists and businesses (especially those that sell goods to other countries) use the metric system every day.

What the United States hasn't done is ban the use of non-metric measuring systems. A country can pass all the laws it likes to encourage the use of a new system, but humans are naturally resistant to change. Americans like their familiar pints, yards, and acres. Until it becomes illegal to use the old system, the average American will stick with it.

In fact, even an all-metric law is no guarantee. Britain (upon whose Imperial weights and measures system the United States based its own) has been struggling with the metric system for decades. Traditionally, the British have preferred their old Imperial classifications, but their proximity to the rest of Europe has forced generations to learn both systems. Recent laws requiring the abandonment of Imperial units by shops and businesses were ignored by a few "metric martyrs," and eventually the European Union gave up trying to force the metric system on unwilling Brits. So fear not, Americans—you're not in any imminent danger of losing your time-honored miles, gallons, and inches.

Q Why is the sound of fingernails running down a chalkboard so freaky?

A It sends chills down your spine. It makes you snap to attention. The sound of fingernails on a chalkboard is like kryptonite to a classroom full of fifth-grade supermen. Children are powerless against it; subjected to this excruciating combination of squeak and scrape, they cannot help but bend to their teacher's will. Fortunately for them, chalkboards in the classroom are becoming extinct—schools now mostly use whiteboards. (Phew!)

But what is it about that sound—that awful, wretched screeching noise—that makes our blood run cold?

Three Northwestern University researchers set out to answer this question in 1986. Their findings were published in the journal *Perception & Psychophysics,* and they won an Ig Nobel Prize (an award that is given for research that takes scientists far off the beaten path) in 2006 for their efforts.

These researchers subjected a group of people to the objection-able sound in question, and they received the same uncomfortable response from each person. They then played three different record-ings of the sound for the same people. One recording had the high frequencies removed, another had the middle frequencies removed, and the third had the low frequencies removed. The hypothesis was that deleting the highs would make the sound more tolerable. To the researchers' surprise, however, the responses of their test sub-jects suggested that the midrange frequencies were what made the sound so cringe-inducing. Hearing the recording with the midrange removed, listeners reported a much more pleasant experience.

That's the *how* of the question. Now the *why.*

The researchers also found that the chalkboard-screeching sound is remarkably similar to the distress cry of the chimpanzee. This discovery naturally led to the scientific theory of evolution: What we are experiencing when we hear nails on a chalkboard might be a reflexive tension that dates back to our primate ancestors. Hearing one of our own let out a danger alert sets us on our guard.

This answer remains a hypothesis, but as any fifth-grade teacher will tell you, there's not a lot of difference between a classroom and the monkey house at the local zoo.

Q Why is it called rush hour when traffic is the slowest?

A The term "rush hour" was coined in New York around 1890, presumably to describe the frantic pace of life in the city. In today's world, it refers to peak times for traffic. But really, could there be a more blatant misnomer? Let's break it down.

First, you've got the "rush" part. Who's rushing? No one. Because they can't. There are too many cars on the road. Oh, sure, there's the occasional bonehead who's weaving back and forth, changing lanes, and tailgating every car he gets behind, as if his manic behavior is going to somehow make everyone else suddenly, magically speed up. "Rush" in this sense refers not to speed, but to the rush of commuters flooding the transportation system—not just the roads, but also public transportation, where finding a seat can be nearly impossible.

Then you've got the "hour" part. The "hour" in rush hour may be even more misleading than the "rush" part. If you live in anything resembling a large city, you know that this "hour" lasts a heck of a lot longer than sixty minutes. In the morning, the roads can start to get hopelessly clogged by 7:00 AM, and they stay that way until past 9:00 AM. In the evening, you're talking 4:00 PM to 7:00 PM. And that's not counting Fridays, when the afternoon rush starts almost as soon as the morning rush has ended.

No, this is not your traditional chronological hour. This definition of "hour" is one of those secondary classifications—a vague, unmeasured block of time. Not unlike the way it's used in "happy hour," which, come to think of it, is not a bad way to bypass rush-hour frustration altogether.

Q What's the difference between a novel and a book?

A We know what you're thinking: A novel *is* a book! Well, you'd be right if we were only referring to the physical nature of a book. While the artwork, script, and colors vary tremendously from book to book, they all (novels and otherwise) are made the same way: The pages are glued or sewn together and bound between soft- or hard-paper covers.

But the similarities end there. A book and a novel are differentiated by the type of writing within the pages.

According to the online encyclopedia, dictionary, and atlas *Encarta,* a book is defined as "a volume of many sheets of paper bound together, containing text, illustrations, music, photographs, or other kinds of information." There are dozens of types of books. Practically all nonfiction works—including dictionaries, encyclopedias, textbooks, handbooks, manuals, yearbooks, directories, biographies, autobiographies, and memoirs—are books. A book can also be an ancient literary work.

A novel, on the other hand, is defined as a long work of fiction. Novels are generally more than two hundred pages long and tell a story that contains the following elements: plot, characters, conflict, setting, and theme. The exception—which is why we used the words "practically all nonfiction works" in the previous paragraph—is the nonfiction novel. This genre, which was formally established by Truman Capote with his book *In Cold Blood* (1965), fuses the stories of real people and actual events with the dramatic twists, turns, and plot devices of a novel.

The word "novel" can be traced to the Renaissance period (the fourteenth to seventeenth century); "book" has its beginnings in the fourth century, when scrolls were replaced by the *codex* (Latin for "book"). The earliest *codices* were handwritten, and many contained the word *codex* in the title.

Today, novels and books aren't just relegated to ink and paper. Audio books have been around since the 1950s, and e-books were introduced in the late 1990s. But while the packaging has changed, the ideas contained inside haven't.

CONTRIBUTORS

Joshua D. Boeringa is a writer living in Mt. Pleasant, Michigan. He has written for magazines and Web sites.

Anthony G. Craine is a contributor to the *Britannica Book of the Year* and has written for *Inside Sports* and *Ask*. He is a former United Press International bureau chief.

Jack Greer is a writer living in Chicago.

Vickey Kalambakal is a writer and historian based in Southern California. She writes for textbooks, encyclopedias, magazines, and ezines.

Noah Liberman is a Chicago-based sports, entertainment, and business writer who has published two books and has contributed articles to a wide range of newspapers and national magazines.

Diane Lanzillotta Bobis is a food, fashion, and lifestyle writer from Glenview, Illinois.

Pat Sherman is a writer living in Cambridge, Massachusetts. She is the author of several books for children, including *The Sun's Daughter* and *Ben and the Proclamation of Emancipation*.

Carrie Williford is a writer living in Atlanta. She was a contributing writer to HowStuffWorks.com.

Thad Plumley is an award-winning writer who lives in Dublin, Ohio. He is the director of publications and information products for the National Ground Water Association.

Brett Kyle is a writer living in Draycott, Somerset, England. He also is an actor, musician, singer, and playwright.

Michelle Burton is a writer and editor with one foot in Chicago and the other in Newport Beach, California. She has written guidebooks and hundreds of feature articles and reviews.

Alex Nechas is a writer and editor based in Chicago.

ArLynn Leiber Presser is a writer living in suburban Chicago. She is the author of twenty-seven books.

Brett Ballantini is a sportswriter who has written for several major sports teams and has authored a book titled *The Wit and Wisdom of Ozzie Guillen*.

Steve Cameron is a writer living in Cullen, Scotland. He has written thirteen books, and is a former columnist and reporter for several American newspapers and magazines.

Shanna Freeman is a writer and editor living near Atlanta. She also works in an academic library.

Tom Harris is a Web project consultant, editor, and writer living in Atlanta. He is the co-founder of Explainst.com, and was leader of the editorial content team at HowStuffWorks.com.

Letty Livingston is a dating coach, relationship counselor, and sexpert. Her advice column, Let Letty Help, has been published in more than forty periodicals and on the Internet (letlettyhelp. blogspot.com).

Angelique Anacleto specializes in style and beauty writing. She has written for salon industry publications and has authored a children's book.

Chuck Giametta is a highly acclaimed journalist who specializes in coverage of the automotive industry. He has written and edited books, magazines, and Web articles on many automotive topics.

Ed Grabianowski writes about science and nature, history, the automotive industry, and science fiction for Web sites and magazines. He lives in Buffalo, New York.

Jessica Royer Ocken is a freelance writer and editor based in Chicago.

Shelley Bueché is a writer living in Texas.

Matt Clark is a writer living in Brooklyn, Ohio.

Dan Dalton is a writer and editor living in the Pacific Northwest.

Jeff Moores is an illustrator whose work appears in periodicals and advertisements, and as licensed characters on clothing. Visit his Web site (jeffmoores.com) to see more of his work.

Factual verification: Darcy Chadwick, Barbara Cross, Bonny M. Davidson, Andrew Garrett, Cindy Hangartner, Brenda McLean, Carl Miller, Katrina O'Brien, Marilyn Perlberg